Carry On Watching ...

A Guide To Britain's Best Loved Comedy Film Series

Stephen Lambe

SONICBOND

sonicbondpublishing.com

Sonicbond Publishing Limited
www.sonicbondpublishing.co.uk
Email: info@sonicbondpublishing.co.uk

First Published in the United Kingdom 2026
First Published in the United States 2026

British Library Cataloguing in Publication Data:
A Catalogue record for this book is available from the British Library

ISBN 978-1-78952-556-4

Typeset in ITC Garamond Std & ITC Avant Garde Gothic
Printed and bound in England

Graphic design and typesetting: Full Moon Media

Follow us on social media:
Twitter: https://twitter.com/SonicbondP
Instagram: www.instagram.com/sonicbondpublishing_/
Facebook: www.facebook.com/SonicbondPublishing/

Linktree QR code:

Carry On Watching ...

A Guide To Britain's Best Loved Comedy Film Series

Stephen Lambe

SONICBOND

sonicbondpublishing.com

Dedication

For Gill and my late father, Ronnie

This book is also dedicated to anyone who performed in, or worked on, any of the Carry On films.

Special thanks to Richard Ross, Carry On historian extraordinaire.

Carry On Watching ...

Contents

Appendices

Introduction

The Carry On films are as much a part of British culture as warm beer and fish and chips. Hugely popular at the box office when they were first shown at the cinema, they have now become cult films, beloved by some, scorned by just as many. While they were made with purely commercial interests in mind, they were never test-screened to the general public, as would be automatic today.

Producer Peter Rogers and his trusted lieutenant, director Gerald Thomas believed that they knew how to make a commercial film, so why did they need the public to guide them? That guidance would come at the box office, they believed.

Talbot Rothwell was to write twenty of the series' big-screen outings. His hero was the legendary comedian Max Miller, and he considered the series rooted in the great tradition of music hall theatre. It is often also said that the series celebrates 'seaside postcard' style humour, which were the comic postcards on sale in English seaside resorts, often featuring lavatorial humour, busty young women and lecherous middle-aged men. This was the territory of graphic artist Donald McGill, who had as many issues with the censors as the Carry On series did. Certainly, many of the tropes within McGill's drawings – as picked up by George Orwell in his 1941 essay about the artist – can also be found within the Carry On series: sex, home life, drunkenness, toilet humour and working-class snobbery. But there are other factors at play, too. Much of the humour and slapstick owes a debt to children's comics like '*The Beano*' and '*The Dandy*'. Absorbed by children for decades, these were staple reading for Rogers, Thomas and Rothwell during their 1920s and 1930s childhoods. The publication of the first issue of *Viz* in 1979, the year after the Carry On series ended for the first time, is no coincidence. *Viz* took Carry On humour from the 1970s, raised the profanity level, and sold thousands of copies.

The main factor that influenced the series as it developed was the style of writing. The team's first scribe, Norman Hudis, came from a play and screenwriting background, capable of writing to order in a variety of styles, in the same way that Peter Rogers – also a writer – had been early in his career. This is reflected in the gentle, relatively naturalistic style of the early films.

When Peter Rogers went fishing for other writing talent in the early 1960s, he went to radio and television. In Talbot Rothwell, he found a man with great experience writing comedy specifically for stage, television and radio. His clients included Ted Ray, Arthur Askey and Terry-Thomas. At various times, Peter Rogers also developed scripts or treatments with Sid Colin and John Antrobus from *The Army Game* and Laurie Wyman, creator of *The Navy Lark* radio series. Tonally, these shows were less realistic and much broader, centred more on 'the laugh' and 'the joke' than on narrative coherence. This is the tone that Rothwell brought to the series.

The Carry On series changed considerably over time, from the gentle character comedies of the late 1950s and early 1960s to the broad, bawdy pieces of the early to mid 1970s via what is, to my mind, one of the greatest sequences of movies in British film history. This period – beginning with *Carry On Cabby* in 1963 and ending with *Carry On Camping* in 1969 – presents a series of comedies of the highest quality. They are silly and broad, yes, but also consistently funny without resorting to many of the tropes and conventions that made the later films far less consistent. More importantly, while most of the very early and very late films have dated somewhat – admittedly for very different reasons – this middle sequence feels timeless. Part of this is because so few of those films were set in modern times, and when they were – like *Carry On Doctor,* for instance – they were set within institutions that function in ways that we can still recognise and appreciate today.

There were false steps within this sequence, of course. Due to the death of Stuart Levy and Nat Cohen's antipathy towards the series, the change in distribution from Anglo-Amalgamated to Rank after *Carry On Screaming* in 1966 was a difficult time for Peter Rogers and his team. Through Rank, there was a move to drop the series name and also to bring in stars that might appeal to other markets, resulting in the unlikely choice of Phil Silvers to star in *Carry On Follow That Camel*. Yet sense prevailed, and the late '60s saw some of the team's finest outings.

Not that a series was even considered when Peter Rogers Productions began putting together a film about National Service in 1958. At this point, there was no suggestion that the film might even be a comedy, as the script under consideration was called 'The Bull Boys' by the great English writer R.F. Delderfeld, later to write *To Serve Them All My Days* and *A Horseman Riding By* to great acclaim. It was Rogers – encouraged by Levy at Anglo-Amalgamated – who decided that the basic outline might work best as a comedy, and after an attempt by jobbing radio comedy writer John Antrobus, which the team considered unsatisfactory as a full-length movie, the final task of producing a filmable script was given to Norman Hudis.

Hudis was rapidly developing into a reliable name in the British film industry. He had worked at Pinewood Studios as a staff writer, but his 'big break' came in 1957 when he wrote the screenplay for *The Tommy Steele Story* (known as *Rock Around the World* in the USA) for Anglo-Amalgamated with Rogers as executive producer. This was a massive hit, and Hudis' meticulous approach to his craft is evident in the pre-script treatments he produced, fleshing out options for plot, character, and joke development in some detail. The treatment for *Carry On Sergeant* – reproduced in Richard Webber's *50 Years of Carry On* – not only shows how clever Hudis was but also demonstrates that he had a talent for collaboration. His work offers options to discuss with the production team, allowing him to produce a script that keeps everyone satisfied.

Many of the other crew were past cohorts of Rogers. Gerald Thomas had mainly worked with Rogers on Children's Film Foundation productions, but had just directed another vehicle for Tommy Steele, *The Duke Wore Jeans*, also scripted by Hudis, a follow-up to the Hudis-penned hit from the year before. Cinematographer Peter Hennessey and composer Bruce Montgomery (composer of the 'Carry On Theme', which was used for the first few films) were also known and trusted names. They were considered safe pairs of hands.

Given the low-budget nature of all of Anglo-Amalgamated's output at the time, many scoffed at his decision to use Pinewood Studios, near Iver in Buckinghamshire, to film the first movie – and indeed all subsequent ones.

Pinewood, which opened in the 1930s, had a reputation as a high-tech and expensive facility, but Rogers ran a tight ship and as well his renowned production efficiency, introduced some innovations, which included locking the sound stage doors at lunchtime, to prevent unauthorised and chargeable usage of the studio equipment, something which must have caused a great deal of anger at the time.

The other crucial factor which made the early films – and indeed the rest of the series stretching into the 1970s – work was the precision with which they were shot. Most participants recall a friendly, businesslike set, held together by the genial presence of Gerald Thomas. Yet it was very clear early on that these were not works of art being produced, but low-budget comedies made to turn a tidy profit. All the films clocked in at around 90 minutes, and most were shot in six weeks, without overtime for the crew or the insanely long days for crew or cast so common in the 21st-century film industry. Takes were few, and small mistakes and moments of spontaneity were often left in the final cut. This is – after all – part of the charm of the series. Of course, extra scenes were often shot and then cut during the edit. Rogers occasionally spoke amusingly of the fate of the wonderful actress Eleanor Butterfield, who appeared in several of the early films, only to be left on the cutting room floor every single time. Later, bigger stars like Terry Scott and Bill Maynard both had their entire roles removed from the films at one time or other.

Carry On Sergeant was a big hit. But how do you create a series? To Rogers, it was simple. You keep as much the same as you can, but write a different story. You use the same production team and cast where possible and, of course, give the film theme music that recalls immediately the film the public loved the year before. *Carry On Nurse*, released in 1959, brought back as many of the cast as possible, but dispensed with the former films' two major stars, William Hartnell (for whom there was no obvious role in the script) and Bob Monkhouse.

Monkhouse might have fitted nicely into *Nurse* – and indeed the series – but his star was very much on the ascendant at the time, and the money on offer was simply not enough for him.

And so it remained for the first few films. Cast members drifted in and out. Leslie Phillips – first cast in *Carry On Nurse* – made only three before moving on, fearing typecasting. Terence Longdon fell by the wayside, probably another early victim of a request for more money. Joan Sims and then Sid James became regulars, as did, in turn, Peter Butterworth, Bernard Bresslaw, Terry Scott and Barbara Windsor. The series also attracted a cast of regular supporting actors, some of whom, like Marianne Stone, Michael Nightingale and Peter Gilmore, made as many appearances as some of the big stars (see Appendix Three).

Much has been made of the paltry salaries paid to the cast members of the Carry On films. Actors would reach a certain level – in the case of Kenneth Williams, we know it was £5000 – and then stay there, often for years, regardless of inflation. After *Constable* Rogers offered some of the lead actors a share in the film's profits, none of them accepted, preferring the security of a predictable salary every six months. This is one of the reasons that Rogers was able to keep his production costs down. He also jumped at opportunities when they arose to use the sets and costumes of other, much more expensive, productions, such as *Cleopatra* for *Carry On Cleo* or *Anne of a Thousand Days* for *Carry On Henry*. He also moved quickly to exploit subjects that were in the news, such as package holidays in *Abroad* or areas for parody, such as spy films or horror, as in *Spying* and *Screaming,* respectively. But most of all, he kept costs low. In Gerald Thomas, he had a former editor who could cut a film in his head, meaning that shots rarely needed more than one or two takes. Not for the Carry Ons, either, many weeks of location scouting. They kept their filming as close to home as possible, as we will see in the next chapter.

About This Book

This book combines fact and opinion. I discuss how each of the films came to be made, but even though I am a huge fan of the series, my analysis is not all adoring. I have placed analysis ahead of irrelevant facts, so some otherwise-fun trivia has been omitted in favour of focus. If I believe a film to be poor, or has some unsatisfactory aspects, or is indeed very good, I say so, with justification. Not all of my opinions agree with the consensus or received wisdom, but I have not attempted to reinvent the wheel and claim that *Carry On England* is a work of genius. It isn't.

This is not a book of statistics, and full figures about each of the 31 Carry On films, as well as the numerous television and stage offshoots, are available elsewhere. My main sources of statistical information are IMDb.com and Richard Webber's excellent book *50 Years Of Carry On*, although some other online sources have also been used. I do hope I include enough statistical information to allow the reader to enjoy the entries for each film. The cast lists are not intended to be exhaustive either, picking out performers who either made multiple appearances in the series or went on to notoriety in other productions. During the book, I call the film by its full title, e.g. *Carry On Loving*, on occasion, but in most cases, to avoid tedious repetition, I have abbreviated titles by removing the 'Carry On ' part, thus *Loving* is more common.

Each entry includes a synopsis of the storyline, which includes spoilers and specific details of the film's ending. This is done on the assumption that the actual storylines are not the main reason to watch Carry On films. However, if you really do not want to know what happens at the end of each movie, exercise caution in reading these sections. Some entries have an introduction which I've called 'Background', but where such an introduction would sit better from a narrative point of view in 'Analysis', which appears after the plot synopsis, I've used that option.

One final point: The Stephen Lambe of 2026 is a better scribe than the one in 2018 when this book was first written. He has tidied up some of the text for readability and clarity, and has updated anything that might require it, which isn't much, excepting perhaps the untimely death of Barbara Windsor. He also likes talking about himself in the third person.

Stephen Lambe, Tewkesbury, August 2018 and February 2026

Carry On Locations

'The movies' have been to the most sumptuous locations on earth. Location teams have searched for month after month to find the perfect ambience for their 100-million-dollar projects. The Carry On team, however, went to Slough.

This is fair enough, of course. These were low-budget films, and it is understandable that the team should do location shooting within easy reach of their base at Pinewood, itself located in the village of Iver near Slough in Buckinghamshire. Where possible, given the sprawling grounds at Pinewood, they used locations within the complex itself. The hospital in *Carry On Nurse* was located at Pinewood, as was the location for *Carry On Camping*, shot mainly in the orchard there. The Town in *Carry On Cowboy* was built on the back lot at Pinewood.

Although the locations for most of the films were within 30 minutes of Pinewood, on a few occasions, the team were forced to travel further afield. To approximate – very accurately, by all accounts – the mountainous Khyber Pass, which separates Afghanistan from Pakistan using modern-day boundaries, the team spent some time on location in Snowdonia along Llanberis Pass. For *Carry On Follow That Camel,* Sahara desert locations were required, so this time the location shoot took place at Camber Sands on the East Sussex border with Kent. For the opening film in the series, *Carry On Sergeant*, the team decamped to the home of the Queen's Royal West Sussex Regiment at Stoughton Barracks, near Guildford in Surrey. Although many of the buildings associated with the regiment have been demolished to make way for new housing, some still remain, including the main gate. Visiting the site is an eerie experience if you are a Carry On fan, and although the parade ground is now a patch of open green space for the houses that surround it, it is almost possible to hear the army boots marching across it.

Two other distinctive locations in Surrey were used when none suitable could be found in Buckinghamshire, close to Pinewood. The Big Pond at Frensham Ponds near Farnham doubled as the sea and coast of Spain in *Jack*. Parts of the shore are sanded, and the author used to visit the Ponds as a child, as it made a passable 'seaside'. In *Cowboy,* during the Indian attack scene, the wide-open plains of Chobham Common were used to convey a sense of space.

The team also made two trips to Brighton, for the works outing in *At Your Convenience* and as the location of the beauty contest in *Girls*.

Urban locations depended on the era. In the early films, up to *Constable,* locations around Ealing in West London were used. The scene where Leslie Phillips asks a jewellery thief (played by Freddie Mills) the way to the police station was filmed on Ealing Broadway, now much changed. The police station itself was Hanwell Library, recently the recipient of a splendid makeover, as seen in the plate section. Drayton Green Infants School became the school in *Teacher*, and still looks largely the same today. From *Carry On Regardless* onwards, Windsor became the location of choice, with several sites regularly reused. A row of houses in Park Street close to Windsor Castle provided, for instance, the office in *Regardless*, the Bliss wedding agency in *Loving* and Doctor Nookie's consulting rooms in *Again Doctor*. Windsor was extensively used in a large number of films, but it was seen at its finest when the Great Park and the Long Walk were used as a backdrop to hunting scenes in *Henry*.

Pinewood Close – little more than a quarter of a mile from the Studios themselves – often served as a suitable suburban location, most notably in *Camping* and *Behind*, and while the orchard at Pinewood was the location of the campsite in *Camping*. The entrance to the site can be found on Seven Hills Road in Iver, again a stone's throw from the studios. Other locations close to the studio were also used for woodland, usually Burnham Beeches, which has good facilities for film crews and was extensively used in *England*. Another favourite location was Black Park in Wexham, used on multiple occasions where a slightly rougher forest was needed, particularly in *Cowboy*, *Henry* and also as the location where the coach stops to let everyone go to the bathroom 'alfresco' in *At Your Convenience*. A few different churches were used in the films, but the 'go to' place of worship was also close to Pinewood, St. Mary's Church in Burnham, most recognisably in *Carry On Dick*, while Fulmer Village Hall was used for two lectures by Frankie Howerd, in *Doctor* and *Jungle*.

But perhaps the most recognisable location in the Carry On series remains Maidenhead Town Hall, which stood in for both hospitals in *Doctor* and *Again Doctor*, and the scene of one of the best-known moments in the series, the Peter Gilmore / Barbara Windsor 'oohh what a lovely pair' classic. In *Matron*, however, an actual hospital – Heatherwood in Ascot – was chosen. Maidenhead Town Hall was also transformed into a university in *Behind*. Once again, so familiar is the Town Hall that it is a rather odd experience visiting it, rather unexpectedly, on a side street in Maidenhead Town Centre.

The Imaginary Worlds Of Norman Hudis And Talbot Rothwell

Compare, if you will, the two different 'worlds' in which the Carry On films exist. In the early years, under the stewardship of Norman Hudis, the films were rooted in reality, albeit an exaggerated one. The characters in *Sergeant* are recognisable, yet it is unlikely that such an extremely poor group of recruits would have all arrived at the same time. While there is some realism in the attitudes of the staff in *Teacher*, it would have been impossible for the students to act in the way they did. While an organisation like Helping Hands in *Regardless* did exist, one suspects that their experiences would not have been as extreme as those in Hudis' script. Most characters in his six films are either motivated by love or by their own character flaws and most of his characters are actually quite nice, really. Even those who are less pleasant eventually see the error of their ways (see Hattie Jacques in *Teacher*). The conventions of light comedy are adhered to. Some characters find love, others emerge better, more balanced and more competent people, and the audience is uplifted by the experience.

However, Talbot Rothwell's Carry On universe is a very different one. This is an adult world – there are hardly any children. In fact, I can think of only one child in all his films – the boy with the bedpan on his head in Doctor –, and even he is a little devil. The girls in *Camping* are very adult indeed, and just as well, as otherwise the entire film would be rendered very dubious. Characters have unrealistic, almost Dickensian names, my favourite being 'Augusta Prodworthy' as played by June Whitfield in *Carry On Girls*. Rothwell's characters are a touch darker, motivated by lust rather than love, but also greed and envy. The desire for sex is the driver behind at least part of the plot for almost all his films set in contemporary times and a few of the historical ones, too. This is not just male desire, of course. Sid in *Camping* or in *Henry* may be motivated by his desire for Barbara Windsor, but it is also Joan Sims' lust for Kenneth Williams in *Up The Khyber* that drives the plot. Whereas 'the story's the thing' in a Hudis script, the jokes are the driver in a Rothwell offering, which means that plotting is secondary; as a result, his films often feel like storylines spliced together. The main relic that remains from the Hudis era is the happy ending, but with Rothwell, there is often a moral twist. Most often our heroes bond in the face of adversity, as in the collapse of the hotel in *Abroad* or the hippy invasion in *Camping* or find solace in a new social arrangement, as happens at the end of *Screaming*. We sometimes end with a wedding, as in *Again Doctor,* but not always with everyone happily married, as we find with *Don't Lose Your Head*. Joan Sims marries the 'title' she craves, but knows she has to put up with the fact that he is an idiot.

Usually, our lustful characters realise that the grass is not always greener, so in both *Camping* and *Up The Khyber*, the characters see the error of their ways. In *Girls,* Sid gets Babs in the end, but at a cost, as the spurned girlfriend (Joan Sims) runs away with the door money from the beauty contest.

Cast Of Characters

Thumbnail sketches of all the leading 'players' in the Carry On story

Peter Rogers

Rogers is the crucial figure in the history of the Carry On series. As producer, it was his relationship with Stuart Levy at Anglo-Amalgamated that allowed the series to develop in the first place. Born in Kent in 1914, his passion was for writing plays, and his career is one of gentle development in the success of his writing, with several of his scripts produced by the BBC during the war, which led to a job at Rank as a scriptwriter for its religious output. A brief return to journalism saw him interview producer Sydney Box, who subsequently offered him a full-time post at Gainsborough Studios in London, where he wrote many screenplays, and went on to marry Box's younger sister, Betty – a great producer in her own right. By the early 1950s, he was producing and running his own studio at Beaconsfield. Although he made several attempts to revive the Carry On series after its collapse in 1978 – once successfully, with *Columbus* – he did not return to film production. He died in 2009.

Gerald Thomas

Born in 1920, Gerald Thomas is not often mentioned in this book, for the very good reason that his direction is so tight and efficient that it is hardly ever necessary to comment on it. Not for him, the sweeping panning shot, the adventurous angles and the intense, directed performance. He was, however, well known for his ability to cut a film in his head, reducing shooting times and sometimes bringing in films ahead of schedule and budget.

A prisoner ofwar during the Second World War, he went on to a career in editing, sometimes working on films directed by his brother Ralph Thomas. He edited one of the *Doctor* comedies, *Doctor In The House*, directed by Ralph and produced by Peter Rogers' wife, Betty Box. His first film as director was *Circus Friends* in 1956 for Peter Rogers and the Children's Film Foundation. He died in 1993, the year after the release of his final film, *Carry On Columbus*.

Norman Hudis

Like many coming into stage and screen writing, Norman Hudis began life working in the fertile ground of local newspapers, writing plays on the side before becoming a staff writer at Pinewood. He developed a reputation for his thoroughness, and in particular his skill in moulding the work of others into good scripts. Having worked with Rogers and Thomas on a fictional biography of pop sensation Tommy Steele, he was asked to pen the eventual script for *Sergeant*. He created the comedy series *Our House* in the early 1960s, featuring many Carry On regulars, before moving to the USA as a jobbing screenwriter.

In the USA he worked on *The Man From U.N.C.L.E.*, *Marcus Welby MD* and many more. He also wrote the popular stage play *Seven Deadly Sins, Four*

Deadly Sinners, directed and produced by Marc Sinden, Peter Rogers' godson. He died in 2016, aged 93.

Talbot Rothwell

Talbot "Tolly" Rothwell came from a background in comedy writing. Born in 1916, he began writing as a prisoner of war, and this became his profession after the Second World War, penning scripts for Arthur Askey, Ted Ray and Terry-Thomas, amongst many others. He submitted the script for *Carry On Jack* to Peter Rogers on spec, although *Cabby* was the first to be produced. Thereafter, his work became dominated by the Carry On series, although he also created *Up Pompeii* for Frankie Howerd. Taken ill during the writing process for *Carry On Dick,* he hardly wrote anything again. Awarded an OBE in 1977, he died in 1981, aged only 64.

Alan Hume

Alan Hume's career is that of the archetypal journeyman, working his way through the ranks as a film crew, culminating in his appointment as Director of Photography on some massive, big-budget films in the 1970s, such as *Star Wars Episode VI: The Return Of The Jedi* and Roger Moore-era Bond film *Octopussy*. His career began aged eighteen in 1942 as a Clapper Loader, in which capacity he worked on *In Which We Serve*, making his Carry On debut as a camera operator on *Carry On Constable*. By *Regardless* he was director of photography, a job he went on to share with Ernest Steward. He fulfilled that role in the last two movies, *Emmannuelle* and *Columbus*. He died in 2010, aged 85.

Ernest Steward

Fourteen years older than Alan Hume, Ernest Steward began his career in film in the 1930s, working both as a camera operator and a director of photography. He became known initially for working on the *Doctor* films for Peter Rogers' wife Betty Box, and was also director of photography on the classic *The Wrong Arm of the Law* before making his Carry On debut with *Khyber*. He worked on most of the 1970s Carry On films, but also had a parallel career in television, particularly *The Avengers*, before retiring in 1980. He died in 1990, aged 79.

Eric Rogers

Rogers was one of the relatively unsung heroes of the Carry On series. Film music is a great mood-setter, and he took the jaunty, horn-based themes pioneered by Bruce Montgomery and gave them added wit. Rogers loved to put in little themes and musical jokes that not everyone would notice, and would occasionally throw in a thematic surprise. Take *Carry On Girls*. If ever a film expects a raucous, big band theme, it is this, yet Rogers goes with a gentle romantic melody, sending up the ridiculous false-gravitas of the *Miss World* competition. By contrast, his terrific big band jazz arrangement of 'Greensleeves', which opens *Henry,* is a joy. In the mid-1970s, Rogers emigrated to the United States, working mainly on cartoon music, but he died in 1981.

Sid James

Sid James remains one of the best-loved comic actors in British screen history. Born in South Africa, he came to the UK in his 30s after the Second World War, looking for acting work. Initially, his craggy looks led to him being cast as a villain, but his breakthrough came in 1952, when he became part of the *Lavender Hill Mob* alongside Alec Guinness, Stanley Holloway and Alfie Bass.

In 1954, he became part of the cast of *Hancock's Half Hour* on radio, where his 'persona', the amiable rogue, was born. The only member of the cast to follow into the television version of the series on a regular basis, his relationship with Tony Hancock developed into a double act, before Hancock ousted him in 1960. Alongside the Carry Ons, Sid also had a successful career on television and the stage, most notably in the archetypal ITV domestic sitcom *Bless This House*. Sid died shortly after collapsing on stage in Sunderland, acting in a revival of *The Mating Game* in 1976.

Kenneth Williams

Since his death in 1988, the true nature of this tortured and contradictory man has become public knowledge following the publication of his diaries and letters. Like many of his contemporaries, he began his professional performing career in the Second World War, in a double act with Scottish comedian Stanley Baxter. He attempted a career in serious theatre, but a talent for voices drew him into radio, where his character 'Snide' became a fixture on *Hancock's Half Hour*. He also appeared in *Round the Horn* with Kenneth Horn during the 1960s. Later in life, panel shows like *Just A Minute,* and chat shows like *Parkinson* became his staple, and he continued to work right up to his death from an overdose of medication. A private, lonely man who craved attention while struggling with his homosexuality, Williams remains one of the most enigmatic – and best loved – performers in British entertainment history.

Joan Sims

One of the most brilliant comedy actresses of her generation, Joan Sims was trained at RADA and made various stage appearances early in her career. However, she much preferred acting on film, becoming a regular in Betty Box's *Doctor* series, which led to her being spotted by Peter Rogers. Only Kenneth Williams made more appearances in the series than she did, but she was not always best served by the parts she was offered; her gradual weight gain led to her being cast in frumpy, middle-aged roles that did not always showcase her talent. A quiet, private woman, she never married despite several relationships. Her acting career continued long after the series ended, and she died in 2001 at the age of 71.

Hattie Jacques

Like many of the Carry On regulars, Hattie Jacques began her career mixing radio with theatre, becoming famous as the character Sophie Tuckshop in *ITMA* starring Tommy Hanley. She also married actor John Le Mesurier. Parts in *Educating Archie* and *Hancock's Half Hour* followed. She continued to juggle theatre, radio and film commitments throughout her time in the Carry Ons, and began a long-term association with Eric Sykes in 1960 (as his sister 'Hat'), which continued in the 1970s in the series *Sykes*, which also starred some-time Carry On alumni Derek Guyler and Richard Wattis. The relationship between Sykes and Hattie became strained on a stage tour of *A Hatful Of Sykes,* and after a period of poor health, which prevented her from getting insurance for film roles, she died in 1980, aged just 58.

Kenneth Connor

Born in 1918, Connor was trained at the Central School of Speech and Drama, beginning a career as a dramatic actor before his physical attributes led to a specialisation in comedy. He made many appearances on the radio, including The Goons, where he was the first choice stand-in should illness strike a member of the regular cast. He also took over from Peter Sellers in the Ted Ray vehicle, *Rays A Laugh*. The Hudis era Carry Ons, as well as *Cleo*, are a testament to his virtuosity as a comic performer. However, during his hiatus from the series from 1965 to 1969, he made many stage, film and television appearances. He returned to the Carry Ons in *Up The Jungle*, though his later appearances were in less sympathetic supporting parts. He died of cancer in 1993.

Charles Hawtrey

Hawtrey had the longest career of any of the Carry On regulars, first appearing on stage as a boy soprano in the 1920s. His acting career also began when he was a child, but his boyish looks saw him cast as a child into adulthood, appearing in several Will Hay comedies before and during the war. He moved into television in the 1950s and early 1960s, appearing in the *Army Game* and *Our House*. Hawtrey was known for his heavy drinking, which led to him being dropped from the Carry On series after *Abroad*, his behaviour having become eccentric and increasingly solitary for some years. However, he carried on working well into the 1980s, mainly in summer season and pantomime, but also making the occasional television and radio appearance. He died in 1988.

Barbara Windsor

Barbara 'Babs' Windsor began her career as a child actress in 1950, and appeared in *The Belles Of St.Trinians* in 1954, before a starring role in the movie *Sparrows Can't Sing* earned her a BAFTA nomination and an entrance into the Carry On series. She also enjoyed a career in musical theatre, winning a 'Tony' for her performance in *Oh What A Lovely War* on Broadway. Her career continued throughout the 1970s and 1980s before she returned to public attention in the high-profile role of Peggy Mitchell in the soap opera *EastEnders*, a series she left in 2016. In 2017, she played herself in a cameo role in the television drama Babs, which was based on her eventful career and personal life. She died in 2020, aged 83.

Bernard Bresslaw

Arguably the best and most versatile of the Carry On acting troupe, 6 ft 7 inch Bresslaw got stuck in two types of roles in his Carry On career: vicious ethnic warriors and gormless nice-guys. Although initially trained as a classical stage actor, he came to public attention as Popeye Popplewell in the sitcom *The Army Game*, becoming particularly known for his catchphrase 'I only arsked'. After he stopped playing in the Carry On series, he returned to the theatre, particularly in Shakespeare. He died of a heart attack in 1993, having not taken part in *Carry On Columbus*.

Peter Butterworth

Butterworth began performing comedy at the prisoner-of-war camp Stalag Luft III with his close friend, Talbot Rothwell. Having enjoyed a successful career already in pantomime, films and children's television, it was Rothwell who introduced him to Peter Rogers, and he made his debut in *Cowboy*. Outside the Carry On series, he often appeared in the films of Val Guest. He was married to Janet Brown, best known for her Margaret Thatcher impression. He died of a heart attack in 1979 during a pantomime run.

Jim Dale

Full of energy and versatility, Jim Dale began life as a comedian in the mid 1950s before a chance warm-up slot led to him being offered a recording contract as a singer. He had a few hits in the early 1960s produced by George Martin. However, the hits dried up, and he turned to acting, making his Carry On debut in *Cabby* in 1963. He continued to write songs occasionally, penning the lyrics for the song 'Georgie Girl' – a huge hit for The Seekers in 1966. Always a very physical performer, he was also something of a perfectionist, performing his own stunts, a skill he put to good use in his post-Carry On stage career in London and, later, in the USA. To millions of American children, he is the voice of Harry Potter in the US versions of the audiobooks read in the UK by Stephen Fry. He was also the narrator of the US series *Pushing Daisies*. He toured with his own one-man show in 2014, both in the USA and Britain. At time of writing, he's still with us.

Terry Scott

A jobbing actor in the late 1950s and early 1960s , Scott was usually cast as authority figures – often policemen. However, he was also cultivating a parallel career as a comic actor on television, starring in a variety of formats, including *Scott On* for the BBC, which ran on and off for 10 years from 1964 to 1974.

However, it was his screen partnership with June Whitfield in two situation comedies: *Happy Ever After* (1974-1978) and *Terry And June* (1979-1987) for which he is best loved. He had a novelty hit with the song 'My Brother' in 1962, in which he performed as a schoolboy, a character he was to revisit in a series of television commercials in the 1970s. He played Penfold in the cartoon series *Dangermouse* until 1992. Afflicted with ill health for many years, he died of cancer in 1994, aged just 67.

Sexual And Racial Politics. Is It Still Acceptable To Enjoy The Carry On Films?

The Carry On films were always intended by Rogers to be family entertainment, and until *Carry On England*, which was given an initial 'AA' certificate by the British Board of Film Classification in 1976 (now changed to 15 in the UK) all of the films were given either a 'U' or an 'A' (later re-categorised as PG) certificate despite very occasional nudity and many sexual references. Indeed, even *England* was re-cut within a few months to bring it down to an 'A' to appeal to a family audience. Yet Rogers played a continual game of cat and mouse with the B.B.F.C., who would generally have two 'passes' at the film: at script stage and before the final film was released. A certain amount of negotiation would occur at both stages, and sometimes the Board would recommend a change at script level only to allow the film without the change at the final stage, when the context was clearer.

The portrayal of women in the series is more complex than it might seem at first. In the Norman Hudis era, the portrayal of women is relatively realistic and well-balanced, particularly when seen in the context of late 1950s and early 1960s Britain. However, romance was a strong element in Hudis' scripts, and most of the younger female roles were cast with the actresses' attractiveness in mind. It is significant that in *Nurse,* all the experienced nurses are pretty, while the quirkier, funnier roles are given to Joan Sims and Rosalind Knight, with their less-than-conventional looks. In *Cruising,* Dilys Laye is on the ship looking for a man (and she finds one), but Liz Fraser is resolutely single, her only romantic encounter designed to facilitate Dilys' love life. In *Regardless*, Fraser and Sims defy the Labour Exchange segregation, while in *Constable,* the female characters are as well-rounded as the men, even if, once again, romance is a prime motive.

We get onto more difficult ground in the Rothwell era. While none of the films can in any way be seen as feminist, among the Rothwell-era films, only *Cabby* features a really strong female lead in Hattie Jacques, and even her actions stem from her husband's neglect. In Rothwell's scripts, women have two roles. The first is as titillation. Often – as in films like *Up The Jungle*, *Girls* and *Follow That Camel* (but I could cite many more) – they provide acres of semi-clad flesh for the male characters – and the male audience – to gawp at. Individual performers are also often portrayed as sexual objects.

Barbara Windsor's screen persona is of the 'nice girl' who enjoys male attention, as personified by her extended introductory scene in *Doctor*, where she turns every male head she sees as she walks through the hospital (except Charles Hawtrey – more on that later). This, again, is a male fantasy and an unrealistic one, particularly fifty years on. Other performers, like Margaret Nolan and Valerie Leon, although given the occasional good line and capable of strong performances when called upon, seem to have been cast principally because of the size of their breasts. In *Camping* Sid James and Bernard Bresslaw travel to the camping site because their girlfriends have not been 'putting out' and they feel a nudist camp may 'warm them up'. Despite their appalling behaviour, the girls – Joan Sims and Dilys Laye – end up giving in anyway.

Bear in mind, however, that most of the men in the Carry On films are portrayed as idiots, albeit lovable ones. Where they let their libidos do the talking, they almost always get into trouble, allowing the female characters – almost always portrayed as cleverer and with a higher moral code – to run rings around them. Indeed, women are often seen as sexual creatures, too. Hattie Jacques' stock 'Matron' character is strong but lovelorn. Joan Sims as Lady Ruff-Diamond in *Khyber* is also motivated by sexual yearning. Joan Sims, in particular, gets a rough ride in the Carry On films, considering how many she was cast in.

For every good part she has – like Lady Ruff-Diamond or Belle in *Cowboy* – there are several more where she is underused or her character is blighted by cliché. The nagging wife in *Screaming* springs to mind, but she plays a similar role in Cleo, and by the 1970s, she is most often a middle-aged frump. Both Jacques and Sims have to suffer constant 'fat' jokes in the series, too. There are still some strong female characters, though. Angela Douglas' roles in *Cowboy* and *Follow That Camel* are confident, competent and independent. However, as the years progress, sexual stereotyping begins to take over, and the ambitions of the so-called strong female characters become weaker.

Race is an issue that we must also consider in this section. It has to be said that all 31 of the Carry On films are very 'white'. There is not one regular actor who is not white, and not one regular supporting character, either. This means that cast members are often asked to 'black up' to play black or brown characters, most notably Bernard Bresslaw in *Up The Jungle*. Also, many of the cast of *Up The Khyber* – including Kenneth Williams and Angela Douglas – wore darker makeup to hint at their Eastern heritage. This practice was considered perfectly acceptable in the 1960s and early 1970s, and although it jars now, context is all-important.

The casting of Pauline Peart in *Carry On Girls* was the first time a black actress was cast in the series in a part that was not an African native, although entertainer Kenny Lynch had previously been cast in *Loving* as a bus conductor – another racial cliché. However, the series really does cross the barrier of acceptability in *Emmannuelle*, which features two characters from India, albeit played by Indian actors. The first is an immigration official, and here the joke is simply that an Indian immigrant could have that job. Later, another character plays a doctor in a ridiculous head-wobbling performance. This does reflect a real shift towards a racist agenda in British comedy of the mid to late 1970s, largely avoided by the Rothwell-era Carry Ons.

So, the question remains, can we still enjoy the series knowing what we know about its sexual and racial politics? If you are reading this book, I suspect your answer is yes. When I watch the series now, I laugh a great deal, and sometimes it is laughter of affectionate outrage. We cannot rewrite history with today's morality in place, and there is so much that is wonderful about the series, to consign it to history for a few (ok, a lot of) breast jokes feels ridiculous.

The Hudis Era – Sergeant To Cruising

Carry On Sergeant (1958)

Distributed by Anglo-Amalgamated
Produced by Peter Rogers
Directed by Gerald Thomas
Screenplay by Norman Hudis, treatment by R.F. Delderfield, additional material by John Antrobus
Director of Photography: Peter Hennessey
Music by Bruce Montgomery
Filming dates: 24 March 1958 – 2 May 1958
UK release: 31 August 1958, US Release: 27 October 1959
Running time: 83 minutes
Budget: £74,000

Cast:
Regulars: Kenneth Williams, Charles Hawtrey, Kenneth Connor, Terry Scott, Hattie Jacques
Regular supporting cast: Terence Longdon, Eric Barker, Ed Devereaux, Frank Fosyth, Bill Owen, Cyril Chamberlain
Guests: Bob Monkhouse, Shirley Eaton, William Hartnell, Dora Bryan, Gerald Campion, Edward Judd, Norman Rossington

Background

In an era when Britain had a full, working, vibrant film industry, *Carry On Sergeant* was conceived as something of a run-of-the-mill product. Conceived by Stuart Levy at Anglo-Amalgamated and one of his stalwart producers, Peter Rogers, as a workmanlike, no-nonsense, low-budget comedy, had it not been the accidental start of a much-loved series, it would now be lost in obscurity. Not that it is a bad film – it is actually a very good one of its type, but one suspects no better than dozens of others produced in the latter half of the 1950s.

Although production notes reveal that Rogers and his team were at pains to distance themselves from it, a huge debt of gratitude must also go to popular TV series *The Army Game*, whose cast at the time provided several key roles in the film, including William Hartnell, Norman Rossington and Charles Hawtrey, as well as some material from one of the series' writers, John Antrobus. Indeed, the subject of both productions – National Service – was a major source of inspiration at the time due to the ubiquity of this form of army training, which required young men of all classes and professions to serve for two years in the British army. The last conscripts were drafted into the Army in 1960, and although there was a nostalgic comedy series looking back at National Service called *Get Some In* in the 1970s, in contemporary consciousness, National Service became a thing of the past.

Also working on that film was skilled screenwriter Norman Hudis, and with a talent for taking ideas, treatments and scripts from other writers and moulding them into excellent, practical shooting scripts. So it was with *Sergeant*, as he took a treatment by R.F. Delderfield – later to be best known as a novelist of considerable talent – which was then converted into a script by Antrobus.

Letters between Rogers and Beryl Vertue, who represented Antrobus, show how anxious Rogers was that there should be no cross-pollination between *Carry On Sergeant* and *The Army Game*. This became academic when Hulis rewrote the script, leaving in very little of Antrobus' material.

That the Carry On team began to come together at this early stage must also have been down to coincidence as much as anything. The four crucial names in the cast list were Kenneth Williams, Kenneth Connor, Charles Hawtrey and Hattie Jacques (in a minor role), while a fifth, Terence Longdon, was to become a part of the company for the first few films. All these actors were experienced character players. Williams was already something of a star, with a parallel career on radio as part of Tony Hancock's hugely popular radio programme, which had also featured Jacques, while Hawtrey had first made his movie debut as a child actor in the 1920s, before becoming best known as a stooge to Will Hay in his comedy vehicles in the 1930s. Connor, meanwhile, had also had a successful career on radio, particularly in comedy roles, while tall, dashing, aquiline Longdon was starting a career that would take him to Hollywood to appear in *Ben Hur* and would give him his own series on children's TV in *Garry Halliday*.

The Plot

- Charlie Sage (Bob Monkhouse) forgets to send in a postponement request, and is called up for his National Service on his wedding day.
- Meanwhile, gruff but kind-hearted Sergeant Grimshaw (William Hartnell), aided by his Corporal (Bill Owen), has decided to retire, and – after agreeing a £50 bet with a fellow sergeant (Terry Scott) – attempts to make this new group of recruits his first ever top platoon.
- Unfortunately, the platoon is made up of Monkhouse, hypochondriac Kenneth Connor, intellectual Kenneth Williams, fey incompetent Charles Hawtrey, aristocratic ladies' man Terence Longdon and guitar-playing slacker Gerald Campion.
- Added romantic complications are provided by Shirley Eaton as Monkhouse's wife, who gets a job at the Naafi so desperate is she to be near her beloved, and by Dora Bryan as her colleague and the hopeful paramour of Connor.
- The platoon is useless, of course, and much comic mayhem is created as they fail test after test, with Connor constantly convinced he is sick and Monkhouse distracted by his wife. Yet, on the eve of their final assessment, they learn of Hartnell's bet, and deciding that he's a decent sort despite all his yelling, they perform brilliantly, pass out with flying colours and win Hartnell his bet.

Analysis

Carry On Sergeant set the tone for most of the Hudis-penned movies, being built around a group of amiable incompetents who rally for a good cause, producing an uplifting – some might even say sentimental – conclusion. It is not hard to see why it was such a success, with a concise and funny script, typically brisk direction by Gerald Thomas and excellent comic performances from the entire cast. Indeed, the characterisations – while hardly three-dimensional – all have moments of depth. There is a lovely scene between Williams and Norman Rossington, playing a supposedly dense soldier who cannot pass basic training, where the former's kindness and patience allow the latter's character to begin to make progress at last. Although Monkhouse's character is our way into the film, he is absorbed into the ensemble within a few scenes, and his storyline plays out alongside the others with excellent balance.

If the film has a standout performance, it is that of hypochondriac Kenneth Connor, who shows what a talented comic performer he was, while the only failure is Gerald Campion, who fails to stand out as Andy Galloway. Both the actor and his character 'type' were dropped from future films.

Carry On Nurse (1959)

Distributed by Anglo-Amalgamated
Produced by Peter Rogers
Directed by Gerald Thomas
Screenplay by Norman Hudis, based on an idea by Patrick Cargill and Jack Beale
Director of Photography: Reginald Wyer
Music by Bruce Montgomery
Filming dates: 3 November 1958 – 12 December 1958
UK release: 5 March 1959, US release: 9 September 1960
Running time: 86 minutes
Budget: £71,000

Cast:
Regulars: Kenneth Williams, Charles Hawtrey, Kenneth Connor, Hattie Jacques, Joan Sims
Regular supporting cast: Terence Longdon, Ed Devereaux, Brian Oulton, Cyril Chamberlain, Frank Forsyth, June Whitfield, Bill Owen, Leslie Phillips, Joan Hickson
Guests: Shirley Eaton, Wilfred Hyde-White, Harry Locke, Susan Shaw, Irene Handl, Susan Stephen, Michael Medwin, Norman Rossington, Jill Ireland, Rosalind Knight

Background

With *Sergeant* such a success, Anglo-Amalgamated wanted another Carry On film as fast as possible. While nobody had any inkling that they had a series that would last 20 years, it was clear that the formula should stay the same. All that was needed was another subject. Anglo-Amalgamated had acquired a play called *Ring For Catty*, a romantic comedic tragedy that had first appeared on stage in 1956 starring (amongst others) William Hartnell, Patrick McGoohan and Terence Alexander. The play was set in a T.B. sanatorium (as were parts of *Alfie* released a few years later). The film uses this basic idea – although this seems to be little more than 'let's set the film in a hospital, base it around some nurses and make it funny' - and gives a credit for the playwrights Patrick Cargill and Jack Beale.

For this film Norman Hulis was required to produce a script as fast as possible, drawing on the experiences of his wife as a student nurse, and his own time in hospital when an appendix operation was needed. The script took him just ten days, although various other writers had a hand in writing dialogue and scenes. Writer-actor John Junkin was paid £50 even though he was well aware none of his material was to be used. Most of the crew from *Sergeant* were retained, as was Bruce Montgomery's unforgettable theme music.

Of the cast for *Sergeant* Kenneth Williams, Charles Hawtrey, Kenneth Connor, Hattie Jacques, Shirley Eaton, Terence Longdon, Ed Devereux, Norman Rossington and Bill Owen were retained for *Nurse*. Bob Monkhouse was reportedly offered a part – presumably the roles given to Longdon or Leslie Phillips – but turned it down, while the film saw the first appearances of the aforementioned Phillips, Brian Oulton, Cyril Chamberlain and a 28-year-old Joan Sims. Making a guest appearance was the venerable Wilfred Hyde-White – cast as the affable but demanding and selfish Colonel – playing up to his usual onscreen persona to great effect.

The Plot

- Journalist Ted York (Terence Longdon) arrives at hospital for an appendix operation. Alongside nurses Denton and Axwell (Shirley Eaton and Susan Stephens) and student nurse Dawson (Sims), plus the Sister (Joan Hickson), are those in his ward, which include: temperamental nuclear physicist Oliver (Williams), eccentric Humphrey (Hawtrey) and outspoken trade union man Percy (Bill Owen).
- Arriving soon after is boxer Bernie Bishop (Connor). On his first morning, Ted witnesses a round from the much-feared Matron (Jacques), the speed of which is also the subject of a bet between the Colonel (Wilfred Hyde-White) and orderly Mick (Harry Locke).
- Ted is offered a bonus for an expose of goings on at the hospital.
- During visiting time, Oliver is visited by Jill, the daughter of a colleague, and a friendship blossoms. Nurse Dawson accidentally calls the Fire Brigade, thinking it is the bell to end visiting hours.
- During Matron's rounds the following day, the accident-prone Nurse Dawson accidentally burns some rubber catheters while sterilising them.
- At visiting time, Bernie shows concern to his wife that he might never fight again, and is later visited by his manager (Michael Medwin) and a punch-drunk colleague (Norman Rossington). A connection develops between Ted and Nurse Denton.
- Charming Jack Bell (Leslie Phillips) arrives for a bunion removal, to be operated on by the attractive Dr Winn (Leigh Madison).
- On the night shift, we are also introduced to another student nurse – Nurse Nightingale (Rosalind Knight), who takes a simple task very seriously, while Bert Able (Cyril Chamberlain) has a bad reaction to some sleeping medication and runs amok.
- The following day, Jack Bell learns his operation is to be delayed.
- Jill and Oliver have fallen in love. Six patients finish off two bottles of Champagne (unusually alcoholic, it would seem) and decide to help Bell by attempting his bunion operation, with Oliver as chief surgeon, kidnapping a nurse into the bargain to keep her quiet.
- Everyone is accidentally exposed to laughing gas, and Percy – desperately needing a urine bottle – has no option but to call a nurse, giving the game away and ending the attempted operation.
- The next day, Bell's operation is cancelled as he has a cold. Most of the patients are discharged.

- Ted and Nurse Denton start a romance, and the Nurses play one last – famous – prank on the troublesome Colonel, discovered by Matron, who smiles.

Analysis

From my rather laborious synopsis, the reader can tell that *Carry On Nurse* is rather episodic fare. That said, it was a huge success, not just in the UK but also – surprisingly – in the USA where it remains the best remembered of the films. Wilfred Hyde-White was very displeased with the final scene, even though the placing of the famous daffodil was very much left to the imagination and no buttocks are shown. The script is full of charm but rather betrays the speed in which it was written, as certain opportunities to develop storylines, rather than just tell jokes, go astray. It would have been interesting, for instance, to see boxer Bernie Bishop's storyline developed into an arc rather than a series of boxing-orientated jokes, and Michael Medwin's cameo serves no purpose whatsoever. The Ted York 'big scoop' storyline is completely forgotten.

There are other problems. The bunion operation scene is – to put it mildly – improbable, particularly as there is no moral justification for it except for Jack Bell's selfishness. A similar scene in *Carry On Doctor* ten years later – with Williams the victim rather than the surgeon – is much better handled, and works better dramatically, although the agony of Bill Owen giving the game away is beautifully played. Although the film moves along at great pace, it might have been better had it stuck with the day nurses. There is a lengthy night-time scene two thirds in, which introduces Rosalind Knight's character and various new night nurses which might just as easily have been rewritten to take place in the day. This is a major flaw in the film and generally characters are introduced and not developed.

That said, the film is funny and the main cast – as ever – are on great form. Kenneth Williams is a convincing both as the stroppy academic, and love-struck paramour. Joan Sims is excellent in her first role, and Cyril Chamberlain is allowed his most expressive Carry On character – his drug-induced frenzy is hilarious. Many of the supporting players are excellent, too – Irene Handl is wonderful as Bill Owen's dotty wife and June Whitfield makes her Carry On debut as Leslie Phillip's prim girlfriend. Of the many nurses on display, Sarah Stephens is perhaps the most enjoyable – it is a shame she didn't appear in more Carry Ons. Until the final scene, the other interesting aspect of the filmis that it genuinely feels like a realistic depiction of a National Health Hospital at the end of the 1950s, and Hulis even throws in a few moments of pro-NHS propaganda – only ten years into its life, let us not forget. Many cite *Carry On Nurse* as their favorite Carry On, certainly the most notable of the Hulis era, and while it has too many flaws to be one of the best of the series, it is still an enjoyable and undemanding romp.

Carry On Teacher (1959)

Distributed by Anglo-Amalgamated
Produced by Peter Rogers
Directed by Gerald Thomas
Screenplay by Norman Hudis
Director of Photography: Reginald Wyer
Music by Bruce Montgomery
Filming dates: March 1959
UK release: 25 August 1959 US release: October 1962
Running time: 86 minutes
Budget: £78,000

Cast:
Regulars: Kenneth Williams, Charles Hawtrey, Kenneth Connor, Hattie Jacques, Joan Sims
Regular supporting cast: Cyril Chamberlain, Leslie Phillips
Guests: Ted Ray, Rosalind Knight, Richard O'Sullivan, Larry Dann, Carol White

Background

By the time the third film in the series came along, screenwriter Norman Hulis was already aware that a repertory cast was beginning to develop. He was put under mild pressure to find roles for Terence Longdon and Bill Owen to maintain the series momentum, and Eric Barker was considered for the main role as Mr Wakefield. In the end, this part went to the hugely popular Ted Ray – already a star of TV and radio, in particular his own series *The Ted Ray Show,* which also featured Kenneth Connor – he was a natural fit. His air of natural – if good-natured – authority was perfect for the role. Mr Wakefield has to be a sympathetic figure, not unlike Grimshaw in *Sergeant*, and this is set out in the opening scene when he refuses to cane Stevens (the instantly recognisable Richard O'Sullivan), the implication being that this is a practice regularly carried out at the school, but one of which Wakefield does not approve. An early exchange between Miss Short (Hattie Jacques) in favour and Mr Milton (Kenneth Williams) – against – confirms this. There is little doubt where the sentiments of Hulis – something of a progressive – lie. The juvenile cast also includes an early appearance from Larry Dann, who was finally to make his mark with a lead role in – of all films – *Carry Of Emmannuelle*, almost 20 years later. In the end, it is a skeleton crew of Carry On regulars that take the main parts, with Owen, Longdon and Barker absent, as was Shirley Eaton

The Plot

- Mr Wakefield (Ted Ray), the acting headmaster of Maudlin School, announces that he will be applying for the job of headmaster at a New Town in Sussex.
- At the same time, it is announced that a child psychiatrist, Alistair Grigg (Leslie Phillips), will be visiting for a week with school inspector Felicity

Wheeler (Rosalind Knight). Wakefield and his staff feel that this might act as a danger to his job application, given the poor standard of discipline in the school. Overhearing this, Stevens (O'Sullivan) organises the school into action, hoping to get rid of the two visitors.

- Grigg falls instantly for Miss Allcock (Joan Sims – 'ding-dong').
- A sabotaged piano disrupts Charles Hawtrey's music class, Miss Allcock splits a pair of sabotaged gym shorts and pointed questions about sex disrupt a reading of *Romeo and Juliet* 'why wasn't we born in Shakespeare's time... Cooorrrr.'
- Wheeler falls for Mr Adams (Connor) in a science class, which ends explosively. The staff realise that the action is planned and, misreading the children's motivations, decide on counteraction to keep the inspecting visitors at the school. The japes continue.
- Wakefield asks the shy Adams to woo Wheeler to soften her, but he initially fails. The staff's tea is spiked with alcohol, and Allcock strikes Grigg by mistake, but they later kiss.
- The jokes become more physical and intrusive, and then the children cause panic by making it look like they are building a bomb.
- Allcock and Griggs quarrel over his 'progressive' book ('I studied in Vienna!'). Itching powder disrupts a staff meeting shortly after Adams has confessed his genuine love for Wheeler.
- The school play is a disaster ('Juliet, wilt thou belt up!'). Wakefield feels he has no option but to cane the ringleaders, but the truth comes out at the last minute, and Miss Short and Wakefield are both touched by their reasons – to keep him at the school – and relent. Realising that he is loved, Wakefield decides to stay. Grigg and Allcock are reunited.

Analysis

The differences between the Hulis scripts and the Rothwell ones are laid bare: 'Are you satisfied with your equipment?' Gym-teacher Allcock is asked. 'I've had no complaints, ' she counters, then laughs, the character recognising that this is a bad joke. As with the first two films, romance is at the centre of two subplots – with Connor particularly funny trying to woo Knight in a sequence echoed, with less wit, in *Carry On Again Doctor* ten years later, due to his spoonerisms, set up over the first thirty minutes of the film. In the other subplot, the first romantic scene between Phillips and Sims is wonderful, due to Hulis' terrifically funny dialogue, so good that it hardly needs the moment of slapstick at the end. Meanwhile, a third 'romance', a love/ hate relationship between William's English teacher, who feels his production of Romeo and Juliet is being taken over, and Hawtrey, who considers his music far more important, is also beautifully written and played.

Indeed, this is quite possibly Hulis' wittiest and most sophisticated Carry On script, only scuppered by the frankly unlikely actions of a group of children who might be seen as little more than a unisex group of St.Trinians students, good though their performances are. That said, the ensemble cast are terrific.

In particular, it is not hard to see why Hawtrey was considered such an asset – he is very funny in every scene, and when required a serious moment when he is terrified that he is about to be blown up, in a scene which stretches the comedy rather unpleasantly, he also does very well. The denouement is also unlikely, particularly Miss Short's change of heart, which is a touch too neat, yet it has the right sense of sentimentality, leaving its audience in the right feel-good spirit.

Carry On Constable (1960)

Distributed by Anglo-Amalgamated
Produced by Peter Rogers
Directed by Gerald Thomas
Screenplay by Norman Hudis, based on an idea by Brock Williams
Director of Photography: Ted Scaife
Music by Bruce Montgomery
Filming dates: 9 November 1959 to 18 December 1959
UK release: 26 February 1960 US release: 23 August 1961
Running time: 86 minutes
Budget: £82,000

Cast:
Regulars: Sid James, Kenneth Williams, Charles Hawtrey, Kenneth Connor, Hattie Jacques, Joan Sims
Regular supporting cast: Cyril Chamberlain, Eric Barker, Terence Longdon, Brian Oulton, Victor Maddern, Frank Forsyth, Esma Cannon, Leslie Phillips, Lucy Griffiths
Guests: Shirley Eaton, Rosalind Knight, Joan Hickson, Irene Handl, Jill Adams, Noel Dyson, Freddie Mills

The Plot

- Due to an outbreak of flu, a Police station run by work-shy, hypocritical Inspector Mills (Eric Barker) and his overworked Sergeants Wilkins (Sid James) and Moon (Hattie Jacques) recruits three new officers fresh from police school, Benson (Kenneth Williams), Potter (Leslie Phillips) and Constable (Kenneth Connor), who join existing special constable Gorse (Charles Hawtrey) on the beat. Benson is an intellectual with modern ideas about policing, while Constable is very superstitious, and Potter is very, very posh. To avoid the sick officers, they must sleep in the cells.
- Their initial work does not go well, as they make mistake after mistake on their new beats, drawing frustration from Wilkins and anger from Mills.
- Also arriving is overzealous new WPC Passworthy (Joan Sims).
- Potter accidentally sets a report written by the Inspector on fire, covering Wilkins with water when he tries to put it out, then accidentally knocks Mills into a pond while on patrol, leading Mills to ban the new recruits from patrolling alone.
- Constable falls in love with Passworthy, and after learning that she is the right star sign, tries to tell her. Benson and Gorse dress as women to catch shoplifters at a local store, but are accused of shoplifting themselves.
- On patrol, Wilkins and Potter discover a wages heist, and give pursuit by car, though the thieves escape. Wilkins and Mills argue that the Sergeant argues for greater leniency with the recruits.
- With Wilkins facing a transfer, he and Sergeant Moon express their affection for each other.

- Potter and Benson spot the car used in the wages heist. Assuming the thieves are still in the area, they collect Gorse and Constable and search for them. Spotting tyre tracks at a local mansion, they apprehend the thieves after a struggle. Mills is transferred, and Wilkins is promoted.

Analysis

Working their way through the institutions, the team now tackled the police force, retreading the rough storyline of *Sergeant,* but with a touch more subtlety in the characterisations. Hudis was again entrusted with the screenplay, although both Brock Williams and John Antrobus had been asked to produce treatments that were not used. Having had an initial, depressing visit to Slough police station, Hudis laid the screenplay aside for a while before discovering the concept of 'Blue flu', which gave him the impetus to continue. 'Blue flu' actually refers to a sort of strike action undertaken by police officers who are prevented by law from supporting union action by withdrawing their labour under the pretext of sickness. In *Constable* there is no suggestion that this is the sort of 'flu' involved, of course, but it's an interesting notion.

The core team of Williams, Hawtrey, Connor, Sims and Jacques are in place, plus Cyril Chamberlain and Leslie Phillips. Terence Longdon and Shirley Eaton both make scene-stealing cameo appearances, and Eric Barker is also excellent as the deluded inspector. Most notable, however, is the appearance of Sid James, giving the first of many excellent performances in the series, here in a straight, but sympathetic role. Sid was by no means a newcomer, though, with a lengthy film career already behind him. He was also famous for his role with legendary comedian Tony Hancock on both radio and television, so casting him in this film was something of a coup, receiving a lot of press attention.

However, all the characterisations are nicely handled, with some of the romantic entanglements left to the imagination rather than rounded off neatly at the end of the film. A brief kiss between Wilkins and Moon hints at what is to come, while Potter's interest in WPC Harrison (Jill Adams) – who we only meet at the start and end of the film – remains promising but unfulfilled.

PC Constable wins WPC Passworthy, but only because Sergeant Moon has pretended that she has the 'correct' star sign. He ends the film still a superstitious man, but perhaps a little wiser.

The four-man team of recruits work well as a group, with Williams nicely restrained as Benson, and Hawtrey also on good form. His opening monologue on flowers is one of his best moments in the entire series and is very camp.

Connor, as usual, is superb, and while Leslie Phillips' suavity does not quite have the power it had in 1959, his scene with Shirley Eaton is actually quite sexy. Indeed, after the starched uniforms of *Nurse* and the relatively sedate schoolroom antics of *Teacher*, sex and partial nudity plays a larger part in the film for the first time, with Kenneth Williams' bottom making the first of several appearances in the series, alongside Connor and Phillips, while Shirley Eaton gives the first Carry On 'bared back' scene, and we also meet one female character in her bra. Yet the film also demonstrates how different men and women fared in the police force of the late 1950s. Moon is office-based – a glorified office manager – and we only see Passworthy outside once, in the excellent scene where *Constable* tries to tell her how he feels, as she walks up onto a rail bridge and out of earshot.

While the plot treads a similar furrow to *Sergeant*, and the film itself is as episodic as *Nurse*, *Constable* goes one step further than *Teacher* and really shows the early version of the series finding its feet, and was the strongest of the films to date, as well as introducing us to its biggest star in Sid James.

Carry On Regardless (1961)

Distributed by Anglo-Amalgamated
Produced by Peter Rogers
Directed by Gerald Thomas
Screenplay by Norman Hudis
Director of Photography: Alan Hume
Music by Bruce Montgomery
Filming dates: 28 November 1960 – 17 January 1961
UK release: 7 April 1961, US release: 1 December 1963
Running time: 90 minutes
Budget: £100,000

Cast:
Regulars: Sid James, Kenneth Williams, Charles Hawtrey, Kenneth Connor, Hattie Jacques, Joan Sims
Regular supporting cast: Terence Longdon, Victor Maddern, Bill Owen, Esma Cannon, Ed Devereaux, Cyril Chamberlain, Norman Rossington, Michael Nightingale, Tom Clegg, Liz Fraser, Judith Furse, Joan Hickson, David Lodge
Guests: Fenella Fielding, Molly Weir, Sydney Tafler, Eric Pohlmann, Terence Alexander, Nicholas Parsons, Patrick Cargill, Betty Marsden, Stanley Unwin, Freddie Mills

Background

If you were to organise a poll rating the 31 Carry On films from best to least known, it is quite likely that *Carry On Regardless* would come last. Its title gives us no information about its contents at all, and the film itself – a series of sketches and vignettes based around the activities of the Helping Hands agency – is too unfocused and gentle to provide the sort of moments that find their way regularly into 'best of' compilations. Indeed, on the face of it, it seems the makers were starting to run out of ideas. While it was certainly true that the series was in need of a new tack, in reality, it was actually becoming the victim of its own success. There was a year between the releases of *Constable* and *Regardless,* and in the meantime two production companies had mooted a *Carry On Doctor* to cash in on the success of *Carry On Nurse,* both in the UK and abroad. Thankfully, neither went into production, but another Carry On was desperately needed.

The Plot

- Six out of work people meet at the labour exchange and accidentally see an advert in the newspaper for the Helping Hands agency, run by Bert Handy (Sid James), with the help of Miss Cooling (Esma Cannon).
- The six are offered employment there alongside former labour exchange worker Sam Twist (Kenneth Connor). The other six are: Francis Courtenay (Kenneth Williams), Lily Duveen (Joan Sims), Gabriel Dimple (Charles

Hawtrey), Mike Weston (Bill Owen), Montgomery Infield-Hopping (Terence Longdon) and Delia King (Liz Fraser).

- They begin their assignments with varying degrees of success, and many misunderstandings and pratfalls.
- A man (Stanley Unwin) visits the offices occasionally but speaks in a strange language that they cannot understand. The team's cards get mixed up, and they wind up with the wrong assignments.
- It finally transpires – after Courtney, a linguist, translates – that the man is their landlord and will evict them, but has changed his mind and will let them stay if the entire team renovates a house he owns. The renovation is a disaster, and the house is destroyed, but the landlord has changed his mind and wants a demolition anyway. All is well.

Analysis

Regardless pulls together almost the entire repertory cast as it existed at the time, although Leslie Phillips had moved on, not wanting to be typecast.

Arguably, he already was. Hattie Jacques was intended for a larger role than her brief cameo as a Sister in the hospital scene (with Joan Hickson as Matron), but illness caused her to withdraw. Her role was rewritten and given to the distinctly more glamorous Liz Fraser, making her series debut.

After starring in *Constable*, Sid James was once again cast – this time in a role a little more like his 'Hancock' persona – as the boss of the Helping Hands agency, assisted by the delightful Esma Cannon. Elsewhere, it is business as usual, with the majority of the screen time going to Kenneth Williams as the vain, pompous, yet sensitive Francis Courtenay, whose language skills help resolve the film's plot, and to Kenneth Connor as the neurotic Sam Twist. Indeed, at times the film feels more like a showcase for Connors' virtuosic ticks and comedic pratfalls. Given less screen time is Charles Hawtrey whose 'Hello, hello' greeting demonstrates that he had yet to develop his catchphrase, and the splendid Joan Sims, while Terence Longdon and Bill Owen are given almost nothing to do at all. With so many individual stories to tell, the supporting cast is also extensive, providing pretty much a who's who of British film acting talent in the early 1960s, with standout cameos from: Nicholas Parsons, Eric Pohlmann – having fun with his sinister public image, Patrick Cargill ('where's the popsy cupboard?'), Fenella Fielding as a wife trying to make her husband jealous, and Jimmy Thompson, showing a flair for farce that was never again tapped in a Carry On film.

The film also gives a second, and last, cameo to former boxer Freddie Mills playing – surprise, surprise – a boxing trainer, having appeared as a bank robber in *Constable*. Mills was to die in suspicious circumstances a few years later. However, the strangest piece of casting is Stanley Unwin, playing the landlord who cannot make himself understood until Courtnay translates for him. Unwin's comic stock-in-trade was the talking of his own made-up 'Unwinese', which won him fans throughout Britain for many years through his many appearances on light entertainment television shows. Here, however, it is a strange distraction, and his three scenes feel like a cabaret act.

The ending – with the final demolition becoming a blessing in disguise – is the most convenient and cheesy of the entire series, but given the film's somewhat fanciful tone, it has a certain charm.

That said, the film is a lot of fun and a little risqué, earning its 'A' certificate in the UK with ease. Norman Hudis once again shows his progressive leanings by having the two female characters 'invade' the men's area of the labour exchange. It is shocking to think that in the early 1960s, men and women were not able to compete for the same jobs. Thereafter, some of the sequences are gently funny without going anywhere much, for instance, like Williams' day out with the chimp, which just seems to be an excuse to send up the PG Tips tea commercials, very popular on British TV during the 1960s and 1970s. Sid is mistaken for a legendary diagnostician at a hospital with underwhelming results. Watch out, however, for the scene where a nurse picks up a phone and says 'Ward 10,' only to have Matron shout 'Emergency' to her, a sly reference to the popular television drama of the time, *Emergency Ward 10*. Other scenes are designed as set pieces: Sims gets drunk at a wine tasting and causes chaos, and – in the funniest sequence in the film – Connor mistakes an instruction to make up a fourth at bridge by travelling to the Forth Bridge in what becomes a spy thriller in his head. The special effects – particularly when he is hanging from the outside of the train – are unusually good, too.

Despite the episodic nature of the action – even more so than *Nurse* – the film does keep some sort of structure. Two set pieces feature all the cast, the first when the team exhibit merchandise at the 'Ideal House Exhibition' (their take on the 'Ideal Home Exhibition', an event in London that first began in 1908), with riotous effect. An underused Charles Hawtrey is particularly good in this sequence. Later, the team's appointment cards get mixed up, with typically hilarious results. Finally, having understood their landlord, they accidentally destroy a house they were meant to renovate, only to find he wanted it destroyed anyway. This is convenient, but it gives the film a nice, round ending. So while it is hardly a classic entry in the series, *Carry On Regardless* deserves rather more attention than it usually receives.

Carry On Cruising (1962)

Distributed by Anglo-Amalgamated
Produced by Peter Rogers
Directed by Gerald Thomas
Screenplay by Norman Hulis, based on an idea by Eric Barker
Director of Photography: Alan Hume
Music composed and conducted by Bruce Montgomery and Douglas Gamley.
Filming dates: 8 January 1962 – 16 February 1962
UK release: 13 April 1962, US release: Not released
Running time: 89 minutes
Budget: £140,000

Cast:
Regulars: Sid James, Kenneth Williams, Kenneth Connor
Regular supporting cast: Esma Cannon, Ed Devereaux, Cyril Chamberlain, Michael Nightingale, Liz Fraser, Dilys Laye
Guests: Brian Rawlinson, Anton Rogers, Jimmy Thompson, Ronnie Stevens, Lance Percival

The Plot

- The Happy Wanderer is a Mediterranean cruise liner, run by the efficient Captain Crowther (Sid James).
- His equilibrium is somewhat disturbed by the arrival of five new crew members, first officer Marjoribanks (Kenneth Williams), ships doctor Binn (Kenneth Connor), cook Haines (Lance Percival), steward Tom Tree (Cyril Chamberlain) and barman Sam Turner (Jimmy Thompson), who has no idea how to mix the Captain's favorite drink, an Aberdeen Angus.
- In an effort to impress, the five newcomers do anything but, involving the Captain in a series of accidents and pratfalls.
- Eventually, the new recruits settle down, and the Captain praises them for not trying to impress him and for showing kindness towards the passengers.
- Meanwhile, Glad (Liz Fraser) and Flo (Dilys Laye) arrive, with Flo looking for love. She fixates initially on the ship's fitness instructor before turning her attention to the Captain, who barely escapes her advances.
- Glad realises that Flo loves Binn – who already loves Flo – and attempts to seduce him to bring him out of himself. This succeeds, and Flo and Binn get engaged.
- Realising that it is ten years since Crowther took over the ship to the day, Marjoribanks arranges a party to celebrate, commissioning a cake from the cook, which ends up full of ingredients from around the world.
- The Captain enjoys his party and announces that he'll be staying on the Happy Wanderer rather than accept a post on a larger, more prestigious liner.

Analysis

Given that they were filmed just ten months apart, and produced by exactly the same team – including the same screenwriter – could any two films feel any different than *Carry On Regardless* and *Carry On Cruising*? Filmed in pristine Eastman colour on a fantastic ship set at Pinewood, created by the set designer Carmen Dillon, *Cruising* feels like a product of the crooning early '60s, rather than the austere, post-war *Regardless*, despite the latter's many good points.

In fact, all was not well within the regular cast. Joan Sims had been sidelined after a relationship with a member of the film crew, frowned upon by the conservative Peter Rogers, while Charles Hawtrey was also out, a victim of a request for top billing and more money. His part was taken by the excellent Lance Percival, already slated for the barman role that, in the end, was played by Jimmy Thompson. Percival's characterisation is a revelation, actually, and while you can just about imagine his dialogue coming out of Hawtrey's mouth, he is a far more convincing head chef, and just as funny. Given his reputation in British comedy, to make only one appearance in the series seems a great loss. Kenneth Williams also felt that he deserved more money, but was pacified with the promise of filming on a Mediterranean cruise. Sadly for Williams, common sense prevailed in the end, and the controlled environment of Pinewood was preferred. Williams stayed anyway.

Replacing Sims was Dilys Laye, making her debut and destined to be a more frequent Carry On actress, but never in a part as good as this. Teaming up with Liz Fraser, her skills as a comic actress were never better put to use in the series. Also returning were Cyril Chamberlain as the Captain's new steward and Esma Cannon, in another 'dotty old lady' role, albeit with enough screen time to earn a few laughs. As for the other regulars, Connor earns a few good laughs as a slightly accident-prone doctor and delivers his own catchphrase, 'cooorrrrrr', on cue. It turns out he has a good singing voice too, accidentally serenading Ronnie Stevens' drunk rather than Flo. Kenneth Williams plays perhaps his blandest character of the series, as the rather overenthusiastic, but otherwise kindly, first officer. However, the dominant performances – on the comic front at least – come from Dilys Laye and Lance Percival, both very funny in parts meant for other performers. In a performance as efficient as the character he is playing, Sid James only hints at the persona to follow, via the scene where he tries to re-create an Aberdeen Angus, and otherwise gives a similar performance to *Constable*. The best of Sid was yet to come.

The problem, if there is one with *Cruising,* lies in Norman Hulis' script, which has plenty of jokes and clever lines ('Si! One of the greatest bull-shippers in the business') and prompted some fine performances from its cast, but could only produce the lightest of plots, largely mixing the storylines of *Teacher* and *Constable* to varying degrees. The result is light, frothy, and, to be honest, rather forgettable. It is great fun while it is on screen, but aside from a few cracking one-liners, it flatters to deceive, as light and fluffy as a Doris Day comedy.

Change was in the sea air, however, and while *Cruising* was the first movie of the series to be filmed in colour, it marked two endings: the final Norman Hulis script to be filmed – a careen in U.S. television would beckon – and the last time the Carry On 'theme' – written by Bruce Montgomery – would be used. The Talbot Rothwell and Eric Rogers era was about to begin.

The Classic Era – Cabby To Camping

Carry On Cabby (1963)

Distributed by Anglo-Amalgamated
Produced by Peter Rogers
Directed by Gerald Thomas
Screenplay by Talbot Rothwell, based on an original idea by Sid Green and Dick Hills
Director of Photography: Alan Hume
Music composed and conducted by Eric Rogers
Filming dates: 25 March – 7 May 1963
UK release: 7 November 1963, US release: January 1967
Running time: 91 minutes
Budget: £149,986

Cast:
Regulars: Sidney James, Jim Dale, Charles Hawtrey, Hattie Jacques, Kenneth Connor
Regular supporting cast: Peter Gilmore, Michael Nightingale, Bill Owen, Liz Fraser, Esma Cannon, Judith Furse, Cyril Chamberlain, Michael Ward, Valerie Van Ost
Guests: Renee Houston, Milo O'Shea, Amanda Barrie, Noel Dyson, Norman Chappell

Background

If any film stands alone within the Carry On Series, it is *Carry On Cabby*. Sandwiched between the Eastmancolor extravaganzas of *Cruising* and *Jack*, the film was originally planned as a stand-alone piece called 'Call Me a Cab'. If you sing that title along with Eric Roger's jaunty theme, it fits. It was only drafted into the series late in the marketing process, presumably for commercial reasons. Filmed in black and white, it has a comparatively gritty, realisticfeel, and far higher proportion of location shots – mainly around Windsor in Berkshire – than most editions of the series.

The Plot

- Speedee Cabs is run by owner Charlie Hawkins (Sid James) with the aid of his second in command, Ted Watson (Kenneth Connor). Charlie is a workaholic and neglects his wife Peggy (Hattie Jacques).
- At the same time as he recruits a couple of new drivers (Charles Hawtrey and Milo O'Shea), Peggy reaches the end of her tether and – without telling Charlie – sets up a rival company, Glamcabs, using their feminine wiles (and no tipping policy) to take over the town's taxi business.
- Despite attempts from Charlie and his team to subvert the Glamcabs business, it looks like Speedee Cabs will go out of business, yet Peggy regrets the decision, and, finding that she is also pregnant, resolves to tell Charlie.

- Unable to do so, however, Charlie finds out for himself and is upset. However, with Peggy's car hijacked by a couple of thieves, Speedee `cabs use their knowledge of the town to head off and capture the crooks. Charlie and Peggy are reunited, as are the two companies.

Analysis

Reading back that plot synopsis, it could easily have been a drama, and yet this is most certainly a comedy, and a funny one at that. The script was written, for the first time, by Talbot Rothwell, in a style rather different to the innuendo-laden scripts he was to develop as the 1960s wore on, although a couple of scenes hint at this. In an early scene with the wonderful Judith Furse, Charlie gets into a three-way argument between Peg (on the radio) and his passenger (Furse), ending with both she and he thinking the other is mad and dangerous. Later, Ted (Connor) dresses as a Glamcab driver to infiltrate the Glamcab yard. While this was not the first time that men had been seen in drag in a Carry On, this was to become a regular feature of Rothwell scripts, although in this case, the reactions from his workmates (great hilarity) are somewhat more realistic than would be the case in later films. Rothwell worked from an initial idea by Dick Hills and Sid Green, best known at the time as the long-term writers for Morecambe and Wise (prior to their switch to Eddie Braben for their classic BBC series in the 1970s), and also used an idea from his own sometime partner Sid Colin for the final chase sequence.

As one might expect from the all-male production team, *Carry On Cabby* is hardly a lost feminist classic, despite the large female cast. Glamcabs use their sexuality – albeit tastefully and gently handled, considering the film's 'U' certificate in the UK – to win clients. In particular, this is thanks to an eye-catching role for Amanda Barrie, later to appear – famously – in *Carry On Cleo*. Yet of all the Carry On films, it does offer the best roles for its female cast members. Hattie Jacques has her best part in the series, and she is excellent, funny and compassionate as the neglected wife and then confident business-owner. There is a great moment of 'business', as she looks in the mirror as she dresses to go out, which is both charming and funny, and may just be her best moment on screen in any film. Liz Fraser also impresses in a decent support role, and it is also great to see the fabulous Esma Cannon given a decent part – and decent billing. Esma seemed to get stuck in 'dotty old lady' roles, but here she has a 'real person' to get her teeth into, and an opportunity to use her native Australian accent.

Elsewhere, the performances are all fairly restrained, maintaining the general aura of realism – at times even more so than a Norman Hulis script. Sid James – while still playing a version of his by-now regular screen persona – is excellent, as is Jim Dale in a head-turning cameo as an expectant father. A high proportion of the laughs go to Charles Hawtrey as Pintpot, playing his usual fey incompetent to great effect. Only Hawtrey could make the phrase 'I've got a leaky sump' sound as funny as he does. Bill Owen is underused, and this was to be his last Carry On, but he and each of the rest of the cast get a few moments to shine, including Irish comic actor Milo O'Shea and character actor Norman Chappell as a union-obsessed driver plus the wonderful Cyril Chamberlain as Sarge – the Speedee Cabs radio operator. This was also the first film in the series to be scored by Eric Rogers, as much a key part of the series as any member of the long-term cast and crew. With so many more location shots than usual, Alan Hume's wonderful black and white cinematography deserves a special mention, and in particular, the massed black cabs in the final five minutes are beautifully shot.

As with *Sergeant*, *Carry On Cabby* is an almost perfect example of a late '50s/ early '60s British light comedy, steeped in the legacy of the Second World War. Charlie Hawkins, for instance, is inclined to help ex-Army personnel, which is how he comes to employ an idiot like Pintpot. A tight script and direction (as one would expect from Gerald Thomas) brings a satisfying storyline home in the usual ninety minutes. While the 'marital strife' plot between James and Jacques was to be repeated in *Carry On Loving*, here the watcher actually believes that he couple love each other yet their relationship has faltered, symbolised by Peg1, the elderly vehicle that Pintpot is given to drive, which ends its life in the final chase, just as the couple are reconciling. As a Carry On film, *Carry On Cabby* stands apart, yet it remains a wonderful film – one of my favourites.

Carry On Jack (1963)

Distributed by Anglo-Amalgamated
Produced by Peter Rogers
Directed by Gerald Thomas
Screenplay by Talbot Rothwell
Director of Photography: Alan Hume
Music composed and conducted by Eric Rogers
Filming dates: 2 September 1963 – 26 October 1963
UK release: 5 November 1963, US release: Not known
Running time: 91 minutes
Budget: £152,000

Cast:
Regulars: Kenneth Williams, Jim Dale, Charles Hawtrey
Regular supporting cast: Peter Gilmore, Michael Nightingale, Ed Devereux, Frank Forsyth, Marianne Stone, Sally Douglas
Guests: Bernard Cribbins, Juliet Mills, Percy Herbert, Donald Houston, Cecil Parker, Patrick Cargill, Anton Rogers, George Woodbridge

Background

For the next Carry On, the team returned to the script that had introduced Rothwell to Rogers and Thomas in the first place. Already a well-known name, Rothwell's work was received enthusiastically by Rogers, and this naval romp became the second Carry On film to be made in colour. As with *Cabby*, the film wasnot originally intended to be part of the series, which partially explains the reason why only Kenneth Williams and Charles Hawtrey were engaged fromthe now-established team of players. In truth, the tone of the film means that many of the regular cast were either not needed, or, like Kenneth Connor, unavailable. The ship was rented from Shepperton Studios at a cost of £700. While still broadly comedic, the crew of the Venus were largely taken from well-known character players, with Donald Houston, Cecil Parker (as the admiral) and Percy Herbert best known for serious roles. This gives the film a strange authenticity, despite the broader playing of Williams, Hawtrey and newcomer Bernard Cribbins, excellent as the hero, Midshipman Albert Poop-Decker in the sort of part that would be taken over by Jim Dale within a couple of years. Also well cast – and largely playing it straight – is Juliet Mills making her only Carry On appearance. Mills was well known to the team having filmed two other Rogers / Thomas comedies, *Nurse On Wheels* and *Twice Around The Daffodils* (which had the same literary source as *Carry On Nurse*) during 1962. There is also a brief – but prominent and funny – role for Jim Dale as an entrepreneurial cab driver.

As well as being the first Rothwell script given to Peter Rogers, this was also Kenneth Williams' first starring role, his past appearances being part of an ensemble cast. While *Jack* has a large cast, the laughs are far more concentrated around the three male principals – Williams, Hawtrey and Cribbins. Hawtrey's characterisation is a touch more masculine than usual – although his character is as stupid as ever – and Williams' character is a progressive, kindhearted incompetent. Cribbins' Albert is innocent, gullible and brave – and just a touch arrogant – but lacking in confidence and intelligence, a typical Carry On hero, with the actors natural talents as a physical comedian used to great effect.

The Plot

- The 1800s. Britain is at war with Spain. With the British Navy in dire need, Albert Poop-Decker is promoted from basic training without graduating to become midshipman of the Venus.
- Taken to Dirty Dick's Tavern he meets Sally (Juliet Mills), who is desperate to go to sea to find her lost love.
- Discovering that Albert has not yet reported to the ship, and so is unknown to the crew, she knocks him out and assumes his identity.
- The press gang arrives, taking Albert and Walter (Charles Hawtrey) – a cesspit cleaner. On the Venus we meet milk-drinking Captain Fearless (Williams), who is seasick, and Albert attempts to prove his identity.
- First Officer Howett (Donald Houston) convinces the Captain to flog Albert, but Albert's vest gets caught in the cat-o-nine-tales and he lives.
- Albert agrees to keep Sally's identity a secret, who has a close shave when she asks for a bath, only to find she is bathing in front of the whole crew, but Albert saves the day, to Howett's disgust.
- With no sight of the enemy and Fearless considered soft, the crew become restless. A Spanish ship is sighted, but the Captain decides not to engage.
- Howett and the Bosun (Percy Herbert) plot a way to cast Fearless, Albert, Walter and Sally adrift by pretending the ship has been overrun. Our heroes fall for it, despite making a meal of the escape, and after some time at sea, they end up on land.
- Fearless is convinced they are in Littlehampton, but it soon becomes apparent that they are in Spain. They steal some clothes and set off for Northern France.
- Meanwhile, Howett and Angel hatch a plan to attack Cadiz, taking the governor's residence by stealth and threatening to shell the town unless the war is ended.
- Poop-Decker and the others find the deserted Venus and fire the cannons, thinking they are shelling Le Havre in France, and Howett is foiled.
- They set sail for home, and Poop-Decker and Sally express their love for each other, but they are attacked by pirates who take the ship.
- Patch – the pirate Captain (Peter Gilmore) – turns out to be Sally's lost love, gone bad. Our heroes are forced to walk the plank, but Sally offers herself to Patch and a battle ensues with our heroes victorious, against the odds.
- Howett manages to steal five Spanish ships and sets sail for home, but spots the Venus.

- Meanwhile, Fearless's foot -which has become infected due to a splinter – is amputated by a terrified Albert. While he does it, the Venus catches fire, destroying an annoyed Howell's new-won fleet.
- Thinking that a Spanish armada has been destroyed, Albert, Fearless, Walter and Sally are proclaimed heroes, and Fearless – now with a wooden leg – gets the desk job he always wanted.

Analysis

Although the film received mixed reviews on release – mainly from critics who felt that the team should stick to modern-day subject matter – Rothwell's script, like many he wrote in the 1960s, is full of wit. The opening shot, for instance, is a perfect reproduction of the famous Arthur William Devis painting *The Death of Nelson* and the joke that accompanies this opening scene, playing on the 'Kiss me Hardy' legend, is a much more gentle offering that he might have attempted ten years later. That Cribbins has to 'drive' his own cab is also a masterstroke. Apart from the early scene at Dirty Dick's, the lack of female characters, while unfortunate, also means that there is a lack of innuendo, forcing Rothwell to rely on puns and physical jokes, and the film is all the better for it.

Tonally, the mix of maritime adventure with broad comedy works nicely, although we are asked to hate Howell a little more than the script allows, so each time I watch the film I feel sorry both for him and for Angel, played by legendary character actor Percy Herbert. The script also gives us a Rothwell trope for the first time – silly, Dickensian character names. Fearless isn't fearless, Angel isn't an angel, Walter Sweetley smells awful and Poop-Decker (hyphenated) is just named after a rude-sounding part of a ship. Care is taken to make sure no deaths are seen, to the extent that when Albert pushes a pirate from the rigging, we hear a splash – suggested he has fallen into the sea. Nonetheless, there are tough moments – Peter Gilmore is genuinely terrifying as Patch in a scene when he is about to rape Sally, and there is another scene when sexual violence is treated lightly, when it is implied that Angel will rape the Cadiz governor's mistress.

So, while *Carry On Jack* did not find much favour with critics at the time, it stands up very well. The plot is ridiculous, of course, although it does make logical sense, unlike some Carry On storylines. Both Cribbins and Williams give fine comic performances – a delirious Williams just before his leg amputation is very funny – and the actors playing their parts straight, particularly Donald Houston and Percy Herbert, do an excellent job, making this another excellent early effort.

Carry On Spying (1964)

Distributed by Anglo-Amalgamated
Produced by Peter Rogers
Directed by Gerald Thomas
Screenplay by Talbot Rothwell and Sid Colin
Director of Photography: Alan Hume
Music composed and conducted by Eric Rogers
Songs: 'Too Late' by Alex Alstone and Geoffrey Parsons; 'The Magic of Love' by Eric Rogers
Filming dates: 8 February 1964 – 13 March 1964
UK release: 2nd August 1964, US release: 10 March 1965
Running time: 92 minutes
Budget: £148,000

Cast:
Regulars: Kenneth Williams, Barbara Windsor, Jim Dale, Charles Hawtrey
Regular supporting cast: Eric Barker, Victor Maddern, Judith Furse, Tom Clegg, Frank Forsyth, Dilys Laye, Gertan Klauber, Hugh Futcher, Sally Douglas
Guests: Richard Wattis, Eric Pohlmann, John Bluthal, Renee Houston

Background

If *Cabby* was the Carry On version of a kitchen sink drama – at least if you squinted a bit – and *Jack* was their take on a costume drama, then where to go next? The route seemed obvious. The answer was parody – specifically the increasingly popular spy dramas of the early 1960s, typified by the James Bond films. Norman Hudis had been asked to produce a script for the film, but liberal views intact, his take was based around a protest against nuclear weapons, considered too risky by Rogers. Hudis – commenting about the script in 2004 – called it 'terrible' anyway. Talbot Rothwell was asked to write a new script, drafting in his long-time colleague Sid Colin to assist him. The result is the first Carry On film to completely grasp, the exuberant silliness that typified the series in the mid to late 1960s. As a result, it is the first Carry On to be truly loved in the UK, regularly appearing towards the top of favourite Carry On lists, even though it was the last film of the series to be filmed in black and white.

The Plot

- Milchmann (Victor Maddern) is a crack spy working freelance for S.T.E.N.C.H led by Doctor Crow (Judith Furse). He steals a vital chemical formula.
- Due to manpower shortages, Number One (Eric Barker) has to send a team of trainees led by Simkins (Kenneth Williams) to make contact with Carstairs (Jim Dale) in Vienna. The trainees are Charlie Bind (Charles Hawtrey), Daphne Honeybutt (Barbara Windsor) and Harold Crump (Bernard Cribbins). Daphne has a photographic memory.

- The four travel independently and make contact with Carstairs. At the café Mozart, Carstairs has Milchmann in his sights but is scuppered by the incompetence of Simkins and team, who are clearly expected and, by luck, discover a rendezvous intended for Milchmann, where he was to be murdered.
- The team escape, but without Daphne go to the rendezvous point later, where Milchmann and Dr Crow's henchmen (John Bluthall and Eric Pohlmann) lie in wait.
- Milchmann is discovered dying, but gives the team a partial clue, and they go to Algiers, looking for 'the Fat Man' (Pohlmann).
- Daphne discovers 'the Fat Man' and they follow him to a brothel. With Harold dressed as a woman, he and Daphne infiltrate the brothel and once again foil the efforts of Carstairs, although they do get the formula.
- 'The Fat Man' is sent after them, with the seductive Lila (Dilys Laye) in charge, planning to catch the British spies on a train. The villains are foiled again, briefly, but with 'the Fat Man' closing in, Daphne memorises the formula, and they destroy it.
- They are taken to Dr Crow's lair, who it is revealed is the leader of a master race of androgynous people. Daphne is brainwashed, revealing the formula which Crow tapes.
- They escape, but fall into Dr Crow's machinery. Lila, it turns out, has been a double agent all along, and demands that the process be reversed. She rescues the team, who destroy the lair, which turns out to be below Number One's office, which is also destroyed.

Analysis

Although the team drew upon the usual faces in both leading and supporting roles, Sid James, Kenneth Connor and Joan Sims were all absent, mainly due to other commitments, although Sims was apparently still in disgrace, and would not reappear until *Cleo* the following year. Kenneth Williams and Charles Hawtrey are involved, however, and both their characterisations are their broadest yet, despite the pratfalls of *Regardless* and *Jack*. Whereas the incompetence of the main cast members in such films as *Constable* can be put down, partially at least, to inexperience, both their characters are irredeemable idiots, with Williams' Simkins pushing as close as he ever got to his 'snide' character from *Hancock's Half Hour*. Hawtrey – as Charlie Bind – Agent 'double oohh... oooohhhh' is a lovable imbecile.

Cribbins is excellent once again playing a similar character to *Jack* – brave but innocent – but the biggest revelation is Barbara Windsor, making her first appearance in a Carry On, having caught the eye of Rogers and team in the comedy drama *Sparrows Can't Sing* the year before. Aged 26 when *Spying* was made, Babs had been appearing in films for 10 years, playing a St.Trinians schoolgirl in *The Belles Of St.Trinians* in the mid 1950s. She is perfect as Daphne; funny, feisty and a little sexy. Jim Dale has an enhanced James Bond-style cameo as Carstairs, while Number One is played by Eric Barker with the ever-reliable Richard Wattis – a veteran of dozens of British films – as his second in command.

One of the main features of a Rothwell script – and this is an exceptionally good one – is his commitment to the joke above all other things. To that end, Barker and Wattis' characters are only marginally more competent than their trainees. The other actor getting an enhanced role here is Judith Furse – most typically cast as an irritable and irritated middle-aged lady. Here she gets a far better part as Dr. Crow, albeit dubbed by John Bluthall, while both Bluthall and Eric Pohlmann are very effectively cast as henchmen.

Despite the obvious send up of the James Bond films, Rothwell and Colin also have great fun parodying the 'noir' genre in general, referencing *The Third Man* starring Orson Welles, with Eric Rogers throwing in a theme very similar to that of Anton Caras' zither tune, while the opening scene which has Milchmann blow up a laboratory and steal the formula, parodies the opening of *Get Smart*, the popular comedy US series also set in the world of intelligence (or indeed lack thereof). Eric Pohlmann riffs on Sidney Greenstreet in both *Casablanca* and *The Maltese Falcon*, while Dilys Laye plays another Carry On Mata Hari following Betty Marsden in *Regardless*. After such a good turn in *Cruising*, she again shows how talented she was.

The film was not without production problems. The James Bond producers threatened to sue, requiring the character James Bind to be renamed Charlie, and, unusually, for the series, the film went well over budget due to the complex sets and minor injuries to Hawtrey and Williams. Stuart Levy need not have worried. It was a massive box office hit. While the performances are excellent – even Williams does not get too close to 'Snide' despite a few gratuitous uses of his 'stop messin' about' catchphrase – the real star must be Rothwell and Colin's sparkling script, which is brim full of jokes, and almost all of which hit their mark. It is hard not to see *Spying* as the first Carry On classic continuing a golden sequence that was to last five years.

Carry On Cleo (1964)

Distributed by Anglo-Amalgamated
Produced by Peter Rogers
Directed by Gerald Thomas
Screenplay by Talbot Rothwell
Director of Photography: Alan Hume
Music composed and conducted by Eric Rogers
Filming dates: July 1964
UK release: 20 November 1964, US release: 22 October 1965
Running time: 92 minutes
Budget: £194,323

Cast:
Regulars: Sid James, Kenneth Williams, Jim Dale, Charles Hawtrey, Joan Sims, Kenneth Connor
Regular supporting cast: Victor Maddern, Brian Oulton, Tom Clegg, Frank Forsyth, Peter Gilmore, Michael Nightingale, Jon Pertwee, David Davenport, Sally Douglas, Billy Cornelius
Guests: Amanda Barrie, Julie Stevens, Sheila Hancock, Francis de Wolff, Norman Mitchell, Brian Rawlinson, Warren Mitchell, Wanda Ventham, Peggy Ann Clifford

Background

If *Spying* was the first bona fide Carry On classic, then *Cleo* sealed the deal without question, becoming, perhaps alongside *Camping*, the most loved film of the series. Here, the transition to latter-day Carry Ons was almost complete. The Hudis-era films have some semblance of reality – even *Regardless* – not to mention a concentration on romantic subplots: even *Spying* has a tacked-on romantic subplot between Bernard Cribbins and Barbara Windsor. However, *Cleo* has none. Some characters are married, and a relationship between Gloria (Julie Stevens) and Horsa (Jim Dale) is used as a plot device. However, for the first time, it is lust rather than love that is the chief motivating factor for a principal character, in this case, Mark Anthony (Sid James).

Speaking of Sid, having not appeared in *Spying,* this is the film where his chuckling, Jack-the-Lad Carry On persona is fully realised. It was to be his main screen persona for the rest of his life, give or take the odd aristocratic lisp. Kenneth Williams also has his finest outing, perfectly cast as a rather gullible and cowardly Caesar, while our hero, if the film has one, is Hengist Podd (Kenneth Connor), the dim-witted wheel maker (he makes them square) who becomes a hero by accident. Jim Dale has his best part yet, although his all-action style is short on laughs this time, something that would be put right in *Cowboy* the following year. Charles Hawtrey is something of a supporting player here, although good value as always.

However, one of the more unsavoury aspects of the Carry On series was beginning to raise its head, with the casting of Joan Sims in a less interesting role, as the scheming, shrew-like Calpurnia and – even worse – Sheila Hancock as Podd's nagging wife. It would appear that in this new Rothwell era, women are nags, shrews or figures of lust.

The figure that is most lusted after, of course, is Cleopatra herself, an inspired piece of casting with an off-beat performance by Amanda Barrie, making her second and last Carry On appearance. Two more interesting casting decisions saw the first of three consecutive appearances by future *Doctor Who* Jon Pertwee giving a broad, eccentric performance and Julie Stevens as Gloria, who people in their fifties will remember as a presenter of *Playschool*, a programme for young children.

The Plot

- British Inventor Hengist Pod (Kenneth Connor) and his newfound neighbour Horsa (Jim Dale) are captured by Caesar's expeditionary force, under the command of Mark Antony (Sid James).
- Anthony reports to Caesar (Kenneth Williams), who has a cold caused by the damp weather. They receive word from Rome that there is a plot to take the throne from Caesar, following problems in Egypt. They return to find Caesar is not popular.
- Hengist and Horsa are sold to slave dealers Marcus and Spencius. Horsa is sold on, but Hengist is unsold and scheduled to be thrown to the lions, so the two escape and take refuge amongst the Vestal Virgins.
- Caesar's stock in the senate continues to fall and with a civil war continuing in Egypt he is unsure what side to take, so also heads to the Vestal Virgins for advice.
- His father-in-law, Seneca (Charles Hawtrey), reveals to Antony that in a vision, he saw Caesar murdered by his guards. The guards strike, and Caesar is rescued by Horsa, who escapes.
- Hengist gets the credit for the rescue, and Caesar makes him a Centurion and head of his guard, making him a hero and turning Caesar's fortunes around, although Mark Antony is not fooled.
- Mark Antony visits Cleopatra and is smitten. She convinces him to murder Caesar so that he can become emperor.
- Caesar sets sail to meet Cleopatra and Antony plans his murder at sea, appointing Agrippa to do the deed. However, Horsa, who is in the galley below again saves the day and Hengist, once again, gets the credit.
- Arriving in Alexandria, Cleopatra and Antony plan murder once again.
- A soothsayer (Jon Pertwee) predicts that Caesar will be murdered, showing them a vision. Antony plans murder, Caesar swaps places with Hengist and Horsa returns, finding his lost love Gloria (Julie Stevens) and planning to steal Caesar's galley.
- Cleopatra arrives, mistaking Hengist for Caesar. Having taken a love potion, Hengist visits Cleopatra, accidentally knocking out Antony, who is waiting below her bed.

- Horsa rescues Hengist, and they take Caesar and Seneca, Hengist having killed Egyptian guard Sosages (Tom Clegg).
- Back in Rome, Caesar is murdered on the Ides of March.
- In Britain, a newly virile Hengist fathers many children, and in Alexandria, Antony and Cleo are together.

Analysis

While the massive-budgeted flop *Cleopatra* – one of the best known and least watched films of all time – is the main target of fun, Rothwell also takes the opportunity to play with stone-age era clichés, in a deliriously historically inaccurate opening sequence that serves up a feast of Flintstones-style jokes as Pod meets his new neighbour Horsa, who seems, nonetheless, to have a beautiful haircut. As the film continues, the main target becomes the much-maligned blockbuster that starred Elizabeth Taylor and Richard Burton, with some sequences – particularly the one where Cleopatra is presented to Caesar in a rolled up carpet – directly taken from *Cleopatra*. Shakespeare's Roman plays are also referenced, particularly in the 'Friends, Romans...' 'Countrymen...' 'I know!' classic line. Much fun is had with Vestal Virgins, jokes about the English weather and – of course – the best remembered line in the entire series: 'Infamy, infamy, they've all got it in for me.' Remarkably, this line was not in Rothwell's original script, but borrowed from an episode of *Take It From Here*, a hugely popular radio series which ran from the late 1940s until the late 1950s on British radio and was written by the famous team of Frank Muir and Denis Norden. Shot in Eastman colour, the film once again shows Rogers' ingenuity, making use of many of the sumptuous *Cleopatra* sets, put into storage only a few months before.

There are, however, hints of the bawdier excesses to come. Sid James – as a somewhat earthy Mark Antony – when offered a busty slave by Spencius (Warren Mitchell in a reference to the famous UK stores Marks and Spencer that had the chain's management fuming and threatening legal action) performs the first of many 'scrubber' jokes to appear in the series. The slave was played by Sally Douglas – the team's go-to 'busty wench' prior to the arrival of Valerie Leon and Margaret Nolan. Aside from this contemporary reference, Caesar's grumpy 'you've never had it so good' comment to the Senate refers to a quotation by Prime Minister Harold MacMillan in 1957, referring to the strengthening British economy. Strangely, there is a moment when Horsa accidentally murders Peter Gilmore's galley master, that feels like it belongs in a different, much more serious, film. Like *Jack,* there are suggestions that Rothwell had unfulfilled ambitions to write more serious fare.

Meanwhile, Amanda Barrie's introduction, halfway through the film, is a revelation. We will discuss Sid James' chemistry with Barbara Windsor later, but there is chemistry here, too, with Barrie. What was it with James' rugged, craggy charm?

There is a lot of plot in *Cleo*, requiring a splendid narration from E.V.H. Emmett, although the story does not make a huge amount of sense, and in truth, it is not necessary to take it in; the jokes come so speedily. Overall, *Cleo* is a glorious riot of puns, Shakespeare, schoolboy-Latin jokes and beautifully over-the-top acting. It is certainly one of Kenneth Williams' best performances in the series, but everyone appears to be having a riot, and Jim Dale pioneers the talent for action that was to see him through the next few films in the series. Composer Eric Rogers also has an excellent film; his score is a continual delight, all perky flutes and ribald brass. There is a superbly clever moment when a mistakenly heroic Hengist is mobbed and stripped by girls, and the theme is played on electric guitar to suggest the crowd reaction to the Beatles. Rogers was a master of musical wit like this, and *Cleo* is as fine an achievement as anything he produced for the series.

Carry On Cowboy (1965)

Distributed by Anglo-Amalgamated
Produced by Peter Rogers
Directed by Gerald Thomas
Screenplay by Talbot Rothwell
Director of Photography: Alan Hume
Music composed and conducted by Eric Rogers (songs by Eric and Alan Rogers)
Filming dates: 12 July to 3 September 1965
UK release: 26 November 1965, US release: not known
Running time: 95 minutes
Budget: £195,000

Cast:
Regulars: Sidney James, Kenneth Williams, Jim Dale, Joan Sims, Peter Butterworth, Charles Hawtrey, Bernard Bresslaw
Regular supporting cast: Peter Gilmore, Margaret Nolan, Michael Nightingale, Tom Clegg, Angela Douglas, Jon Pertwee, Sally Douglas
Guests: Sidney Bromley, Brian Rawlinson, Davy Kaye, Percy Herbert, Edina Ronay, Alan Gifford, Brian Coburn, Eric Rogers

Background

I would argue that not only is *Carry On Cowboy* the finest of all 31 Carry On films, but that it is the best Western parody ever made. It's more consistently funny – for instance – than the much-lauded Mel Brooks film *Blazing Saddles*, while the other close runners – like the Bob Hope *Paleface* and *Son Of Paleface* and the early 1960s Jane Fonda vehicle *Cat Balou* have dated somewhat more than *Carry On Cowboy*. Indeed, when the first planning meetings took place at the start of 1965, there was some concern that The Beatles were about to make a western parody, but thankfully, such fears were allayed as the script for *Help* seemed more to their liking.

The Plot

- Outlaw The Rumpo Kid (Sid James) takes over sleepy Western Town Stodge City run by lazy Judge Burke (Kenneth Williams).
- He develops partnerships with Belle (Joan Sims), the local saloon owner, and her barman, Charlie (Percy Herbert), who becomes Rumpo's chief lieutenant.
- In taking over the town, they murder the incompetent sheriff, Albert Earp (Jon Pertwee).
- Judge Burke sends for a US Marshall, a job accidentally given to an English sanitation engineer, Marshall P. Nutt (Jim Dale), while simultaneously Earp's daughter Annie Oakley (Angela Douglas) arrives to avenge her father's death.
- All manner of japes ensue, some involving the local Indian tribe, led by Big Heap (Charles Hawtrey), until Marshall finally wins out with his sanitation skills and some shooting ability taught by Annie, and gets the girl.

- Rumpo and Belle escape at the last minute.

Analysis

The film is a hoot from start to finish, sustaining itself even though its middle third, when so many comedies – and many a Carry On – lose their way. Playing parts somewhat removed from the stock characters they are developing elsewhere in the series, many of the cast – like Sid James and Joan Sims – are clearly having great fun with their roles. However, it is the central conceit of the film – that a English sanitation engineer (1st class) played with engaging hilarity and huge energy by Jim Dale – can be mistaken for a US Marshall because of his Christian name and asked to 'clean up' Stodge City – that gives the film it's spine, allowing the comic scenes to mean something, rather than just delivering a jumping off point for a series of sketches. Dale had impressed in smaller, straighter roles in previous films, including *Cabby* and *Spying,* but his terrific performance in *Cowboy* really propels the film, and was acknowledged at the time by both Michael Sullivan, Sid James' agent and Keith Devon, a Director at Bernard Delfont's agency, both of whom saw Dale as a star in the making.

Western films – and TV series – were still at the height of their popularity in the early '60s, and *Carry On Cowboy* takes many of its cues from classic Westerns like High Noon, from which its denouement is borrowed, and series like *Bonanza* and *Gunsmoke*. While the sets built at Pinewood are splendid and superbly crafted – worth every penny of the movie's budget – it is clear that research for Talbot Rothwell's otherwise-excellent script had gone no further than a few movies and TV shows.

But no matter – the cast are clearly having a ball, with Joan Sims – in her most glamorous Carry On role by far – and the rest of the cast revelling in their characterisations. Sid James plays his part as a mixture of Humphrey Bogart and Gary Cooper, while Kenneth Williams supposedly based his character of the Judge on film producer Hal Roach (although I can find no comparative evidence for this), requiring him to talk out of one side of his face, leading to some muscular problems as filming wore on. Making her debut was Angela Douglas in the sort of glamorous, traditional 'female juvenile lead' role preferred in the series until the late '60s when Barbara Windsor's sexy/funny persona became the norm, and Anita Harris and Jacki Piper took over these parts in lesser roles as the series wore on. Also appearing for the first time were Peter Butterworth, who was already well known on both adult and children's TV – excellent as Judge Burke's sidekick Doc – and Bernard Bresslaw as Little Heap, while Sydney Bromley made his only Series appearance as put-upon, big-bearded rancher Sam Houston, a role he was seemingly born to play. Other notable appearances were from '60s starlet Edina Ronay as Dolores, now a fashion designer, who plays the showgirl who becomes – briefly – part of a love quadrangle also involving Marshall, Annie Oakley and Belle. Also appearing was Brian Rawlinson – very funny as the stagecoach guard, Davy Kaye as the ever-enthusiastic undertaker, Josh and – in her first 'busty crumpet' Carry On role – Margaret Nolan.

And then there is Charles Hawtrey, as the whiskey-obsessed Big Heap. Despite the commitment made by many of the other actors to attempt accents, Hawtrey plays his character as... Charles Hawtrey ('Oh...hellooooo'). Of course, within the context of the Carry On series, this works just fine, but for anyone watching in (say) the USA, this bizarre characterisation will have mystified them completely, which is probably one of the reasons the film is rarely discussed in the litany of classic Western comedies.

A test of a good Carry On is how many of the sequences still work, and one of the best things about *Carry On Cowboy* is that the majority of the film holds up well. A few sequences still jar. The most obvious one is the 'cat fight' sequence – where Sims, Douglas and Ronay fight – literally – for Marshall's affections.

This scene is brief but poor, and includes some dubbed-on tearing sounds since the women barely seem to be touching each other. Jon Pertwee's myopic and almost deaf sheriff is also a little tedious, and there are only so many laughs you can get from someone bumping into things. In terms of morality, this was the least 'innocent' of the Series yet, justifying the films 'A' certificate with ease. The film is saucy – the Can-Can scene is more than risqué, for instance, and the number of deaths is very high for a Carry On. Additionally, the scene where Marshall is almost lynched is actually fairly tough, despite the dialogue's flippancy. Charlie's death – shot by Annie by mistake – is also played for laughs despite the only moral justification being that he is part of Rumpo's gang.

While Marshall gets the girl in the end, the Rumpo Kid is allowed to escape. No matter how bad Sid's character has been in any film, he always emerges, bruised and battered sometimes, but in one piece.

Despite these minor missteps, almost everything else hits the mark. There is a montage scene, for instance, just before the finale, where Annie teaches Marshall how to shoot, that is as funny as anything comparable in a Woody Allen movie, while the physical comedy from Dale in the stagecoach attack is priceless. James and Sims are first-rate, and Williams sustains his accent and performance remarkably well, considering the relative paucity of the role. The locations – Black Park near Pinewood and on Chobham Common in Surrey, masquerading as the open prairies of the old west – pass muster well, and the costumes are sumptuous and well researched. I particularly enjoyed Sidney Bromley's Confederate jacket.

Contemporary reviews largely agreed with mine, and even Kenneth Williams – usually prone to dismissing the Carry On scripts – praised it in his diaries while *The Sunday Times* classed it a 'corker by any standards'. Some reviewers commented on its darker tone and in a more recent review *Empire Magazine* classed it 'easily the franchise's darkest hour', citing both the Rumpo Kid and Annie Oakley's bloodthirsty nature. That *Carry On Cowboy* remains – arguably, of course – the best Carry On film is not just down to a good script, great performances, and inspired subject matter. The series itself had reached a peak via *Spying* and *Cleo*, and while the next three films were to continue the historical theme, none of them – for one reason or another – quite reached the heights of this classic.

Carry On Screaming! (1966)

Distributed by Anglo-Amalgamated
Produced by Peter Rogers
Directed by Gerald Thomas
Screenplay by Talbot Rothwell
Director of Photography: Alan Hume
Music composed and conducted by Eric Rogers
Song: 'Carry On Screaming' by Myles Rudge and Ted Dick
Filming dates: 10 January 1966 – 25 February 1966
UK Release: 19 August 1966, US release: 7 April 1967
Running time: 97 minutes
Budget: £197,500

Cast:
Regulars: Kenneth Williams, Jim Dale, Joan Sims, Peter Butterworth, Charles Hawtrey, Bernard Bresslaw
Regular supporting cast: Tom Clegg, Frank Forsyth, Sally Douglas, Angela Douglas, Michael Ward, Marianne Stone, Billy Cornelius, Jon Pertwee
Guests: Harry H.Corbett, Frank Thornton, Fenella Fielding, Norman Mitchell

Background

With *Cowboy* another box-office winner and parody the name of the game, the target the team chose next was horror. Rothwell approached his subject with glee. Several sources for parody were available from the outset, with both *The Munsters* and *The Addams Family* in current production and shown on British television. Even though both were short-lived runs – ending in 1966 – these high-concept situation comedies were proving popular with audiences on both sides of the Atlantic. Rothwell drew characters from both series, with Bernard Bresslaw a credible Lurch (*The Addams Family*) despite never having seen the show, and Fenella Fielding – in her second and last Carry On – drawing both on Morticia Adams and Lily Munster. However, it is the late 1950s and early 1960s horror movies from Hammer Studios on which Rothwell draws most closely, while cinematographer Alan Hume creates a superb facsimile of the Hammer tone with his fabulously moody colour camerawork.

The Plot

- Courting in the woods with her boyfriend, Albert Potter (Jim Dale), Doris Mann (Angela Douglas) is kidnapped by a large, hairy creature, Odbodd (Tom Clegg), in the same location where five other women have gone missing
- Albert reports the news to the police and Sergeant Bung (Harry H.Corbett) and Constable Slobotham (Peter Butterworth) investigate. A disembodied finger has been found at the scene.
- They spot Odbodd and follow him to a mansion, 'Bide-a-wee' rest home,

where they meet the dead (but regenerating) Doctor Watt (Kenneth Williams). Watt behaves oddly, then vanishes, and the investigators flee.

- It is revealed that Doris is indeed at the mansion.
- Dr Fettle (Jon Pertwee) examines the finger, revealing that it comes from a long-extinct creature.
- Bung, Slobotham and Potter follow a lead to a local public convenience to see Dan Dann (The Lavatory Man, played by Charles Hawtrey), who used to work for Watt and his sister Virula (Fenella Fielding). Watt and Virula secretly follow.
- Odbodd murders Dan just as he is about to complete his story, and after regenerating Odbodd junior (Billy Cornelius) from the finger, Dr Fettle is also murdered.
- Bung returns to 'Bide-a-wee' alone and is enamoured by Virula, finally giving in to her charms.
- The following morning, Potter discovers a mannequin in a shop that he is convinced is Doris. He is not believed. It is revealed that the kidnapped girls are being coated with a hard-drying chemical and then sold as dummies.
- The infatuated Bung returns once again to see Virula, telling her about the dummy sighting.
- Watt and Virula decide to retrieve the Doris dummy, which they get Bung to do, after Virula gives him a potion, transforming him into a Mr. Hyde-type creature.
- He returns home as the creature but is still no match for his nagging wife (Joan Sims), and wakes up in the bath, back to his normal self, with no memory of his actions.
- The dummy theft is investigated, and footprints are found. Potter is arrested under suspicion of stealing the dummy, but has too many toes to match the creature that committed the crime.
- Bung decides to set a trap, placing Slobotham as a lure, dressed as a woman. Bung's wife follows, suspecting him of having an affair.
- The two Odbodds go hunting and Potter also investigates carrying a shotgun. Mrs. Bung is abducted, as is Slobotham.
- Watt continues his pet project – to revive an Egyptian mummy.
- They begin to work on Mrs Bung and realise that Slobotham is a man. Bung and Potter arrive and a plot is hatched to kill them, sending a snake to kill them while they sleep, but Bung shoots it.
- The two Odbodds chase them, but they have a lucky escape into the basement, where they rescue Slobotham and Doris, and discover Mrs Bung.
- Potter accidentally takes the same potion as Bung earlier, attacking the two Odbodds and saving everyone.
- The Mummy revives during a storm, attacking Watt who falls into a vat of his own chemicals.
- Potter and Doris marry, and we find Bung and Virula together, with Mrs Bung still a dummy.

Analysis

Casting was to become the main issue for critics, with Jim Dale, Angela Douglas, Joan Sims and even Kenneth Williams given reduced screen time in favour of two well-cast guest stars. The pouting Fenella Fielding is perfectly cast as the vampish – and vampirish – Virula Watt. However, it was the casting of Harry H. Corbett – not currently engaged in his best-known role as Albert in *Steptoe And Son* – that caused the most controversy at the time. He was brought in by Rogers to play the main protagonist, the enthusiastic but less than competent Sergeant Bung, at a massive fee of £12,000 – then a record for the series. The part had originally been written for Sid James, yet it is hard to imagine Sid in the role. Whether playing an authority figure or a lecher, Sid usually plays characters with a certain level of competence, while Corbett's Bung is a deluded figure, no more competent than his sidekick, Slobotham, but with delusions of grandeur. Some critics at the time felt Corbett's performance was a little too broad even for the Carry On series, but I rather like his eccentric performance, clearly modelled on a Sherlock Holmes-type character.

Rothwell is again in his element, poking fun not just at the horror genre, but also at late Victorian and Edwardian values. In the first five minutes, there are jokes about long, frustrating courtships (from the male point of view) and the new-fangled telephone. Much Abbott and Costello-style fun is had with Doctor Watt's name, aping their notorious 'who's on first' sketch. Virula's smoking scene is another classic Carry On moment. Both Sherlock Holmes and also Dr. Jeckyl and Mr. Hyde are sent-up – the scene where Bung and Potter are attacked by a snake borrowed from the Holmes story 'The Speckled Band'.

Once again, the wit of composer Eric Rogers is demonstrated, throwing in the theme to *Z Cars*, the long-running British police drama, whenever Bung drives his car, plus the theme to *Steptoe And Son* when, as the Mr Hyde-type creature, he rides a horse and cart.

What is frustrating about *Screaming* is the sidelining – indeed, in some cases, wasting – of its cast of regulars. Kenneth Williams gets a few decent lines, particularly his climactic 'Frying Tonight', while Joan Sims is again cast as a nag, and Angela Douglas has almost nothing to do, spending most of the film as an inanimate dummy. Jim Dale, after his triumphant turn in *Cowboy*, has a little more action, but is largely a sidekick to Corbett. After an eye-catching small role in *Cowboy*, Peter Butterworth is excellent in an enhanced role, working well with Corbett, while Bernard Bresslaw also impresses in the tiny part as the Lurch-like butler. Jon Pertwee gives a typically eccentric performance in a small 'nutty professor' role, and Charles Hawtrey – cast at the last minute – gives, in my opinion, his best performance in a Carry On as the house-proud toilet attendant. But the film really belongs to Corbett and Fielding, which may not sit well with fans of the regulars, but it does make for an entertaining, fast-moving film.

Carry On ... Don't Lose Your Head (1966)

Distributed by Rank
Produced by Peter Rogers
Directed by Gerald Thomas
Screenplay by Talbot Rothwell
Director of Photography: Alan Hume
Music composed and conducted by Eric Rogers
Song: 'Don't Lose Your Head' by Bill Martin and Phil Couter
Filming dates: 12 September 1966 – 28 October 1966
UK release: 2 March 1967, US release: 14 December 1967
Running time: 90 minutes
Budget: £200,000

Cast:
Regulars: Sid James, Kenneth Williams, Jim Dale, Joan Sims, Peter Butterworth, Charles Hawtrey
Regular supporting cast: Peter Gilmore, Marianne Stone, Valerie Van Ost, Michael Nightingale, Julian Orchard, Michael Ward, Billy Cornelius, Hugh Futcher, David Davenport, Billy Cornelius
Guests: Danny Robin, Jacqueline Pearce, Ronnie Brody, Patrick Allen

The Plot

- In Paris, the Reign of Terror during the French Revolution is in full swing, presided over by Citizens Camembert and Bidet (Kenneth Williams and Peter Butterworth).
- Meanwhile, in England, Sir Rodney Ffing (Sid James) and Lord Darcy (Jim Dale), hearing of the carnage, decide to help out of boredom, with Ffing becoming 'The Black Fingernail'.
- Robespierre (Peter Gilmore) is furious with the disruption the Fingernail is causing. The next Aristocrat due to die is the high-profile Duc de Pommfrit (Charles Hawtrey), who is rescued by Ffing and Darcy.
- Robespierre is even more furious, ordering Camembert to find The Fingernail or face execution. Ffing appears dressed as a woman, and is allowed to go, only for Camembert to realise too late that it was the Fingernail .
- They rush to Calais to attempt to cut him off, but their coach is actually driven by Ffing and Darcy, both in disguise. To get Pommfrit away, Ffing creates a diversion, stumbling upon Jacqueline (Dany Robin).
- The pair are immediately attracted to each other, and she creates a distraction to allow him to escape, pretending to be the Fingernail. Her sex is revealed in front of Robespierre, who is furious, sending Camembert and Bidet to England. They travel as aristocrats with Camembert's sister Desiree (Joan Sims), who wants to marry an aristocrat, despite the Revolution.
- From the girl, they find a silver locket with teeth in, which they believe is a clue to the identity of the Fingernail. The teeth actually belong to Ffing's mother.

- Hearing that they are in England, Darcy invites them to a ball put on by Ffing. They arrive and search for clues to the Fingernail's identity, while Ffing also tries to identify Camembert. Pommfrit is also at the party. He and Desiree rendezvous in the arbour, and she attempts to discover the identity of the Fingernail, hinting at sexual favours. Bidet watches.
- Ffing and Darcy, sure of his identity now, taunt Camembert. Desiree also meets Ffing, who promises to marry her if she does not reveal that he is the Fingernail and tell him where Jacqueline is being held.
- Camembert finds them embracing in the arbour, and challenges Ffing to a duel at dawn. Ffing manoeuvres Camembert into a cesspit.
- The action returns to Paris as Ffing and Darcy return to rescue Jacqueline, but Camembert moves her to another location – Chateaux Neuf. Ffing, Darcy and Pommfrit overhear the plan, but not the location, so contrive to get the information with Ffing disguised as Robespierre.
- Camembert, Bidet and Desiree rush to the Chateaux, observed by our heroes. Camembert admires the artworks in the Chateaux, while Ffing attempts to blow their way in. Bidet opens the door at the last minute, so our heroes sense a trap, and elect to catapult Ffing into the house instead.
- He lands in Desiree's room and convinces her to help him. She sneaks him out of the room and into Jacqueline's under a large dress. Darcy and Pommfrit arrive and a fight ensues while Camembert tries to protect the artworks.
- In the end, our heroes win and the Chateaux is completely destroyed. Robespierre has Camembert and Bidet executed, with Ffing operating the guillotine. Ffing marries Jacqueline and Pommfrit marries a less than happy Desiree.

Analysis

Following *Screaming* and the death of Stuart Levy, Anglo-Amalgamated ended their association with the Carry On series, chasing classier fare, according to Rogers, so he offered the next film to Rank. However, the new distributors were nervous about using another company's brand, and so the Carry On moniker was dropped for the next two films, before being reinstated for television showings after 1968. The marketing team still used the series title in the advertising blurb, lest there be any doubt about what viewers were watching. There were also issues about using *The Scarlet Pimpernel* since Baroness Orczy's novels were still in copyright until the 1970s, so an inspired alternative name, 'The Black Fingernail' was invented, despite the character being exactly the same as Pimpernel in all but name.

As for the film itself, Rogers – optimistic and opportunistic as ever – asserted that the all-action nature of the movie would allow it to stand out from the series as a different sort of film. He was wrong, of course. Despite the swash-buckling nature of the last fifteen minutes, this is a Carry On through and through, with all the regulars present with puns at the ready. Rothwell excels himself once again with a script rich with jokes, often at the expense of the

French language. 'I am citizen Camembert. I am the big cheese' exclaims Kenneth Williams, who once again gets most of the best lines. Indeed, if you like your Carry On characters to have silly – and slightly risqué names – then characters like Camembert, Pommfrit, Malebonce, Bidet and Ffing will make you roar with laughter. Sid James and Jim Dale make a fine pair of heroes, and while we expect all-action from Dale, Sid's agility in the final fight scene is very impressive, particularly as he was to have a heart attack only a few months later.

After a poor role in *Screaming* Joan Sims is much better served here, having great fun with a faux-posh accent in one of her best Carry On performances. Dany Robin – an actress very well known in France but almost unknown in Britain – plays Sid's love interest engagingly. Given that the entire cast play their roles with their normal accents, her French one is actually rather incongruous. Peter Gilmore – in his best Carry On role – is splendid as Robespierre.

The film really benefits from a terrific ball sequence, which looks – and was – expensive and takes up nearly half an hour of the film. As well as advancing the plot, there are plenty of laughs, with Sims a particular delight. For the only time in a Carry On film (except the odd aside from Frankie Howerd in later films), Rothwell throws in some 'asides' to the camera, as characters share their innermost thoughts with us, wittily copying this convention of stage drama from Shakespeare onwards.

Some of the interiors for this sequence were filmed at Clandon Park in Surrey, sadly lost to fire in 2015.

The duel sequence is also a hoot, with Hawtrey very funny, refereeing the duel as a football match. Only the final action sequence fails to convince. Although Dale, James and even Hawtrey are all excellent, some less-than-convincing stunts and special effects let the side down, in one of the only sequences in the entire series when Gerald Thomas' direction and the editing come up short. The joke here – that the fight causes such chaos that priceless artworks and finally the house itself are destroyed – is neither particularly funny nor particularly well (for want of a better word) executed. But having said that, *Don't Lose Your Head* is still a very decent edition of the series, and well worth an hour and a half of your time.

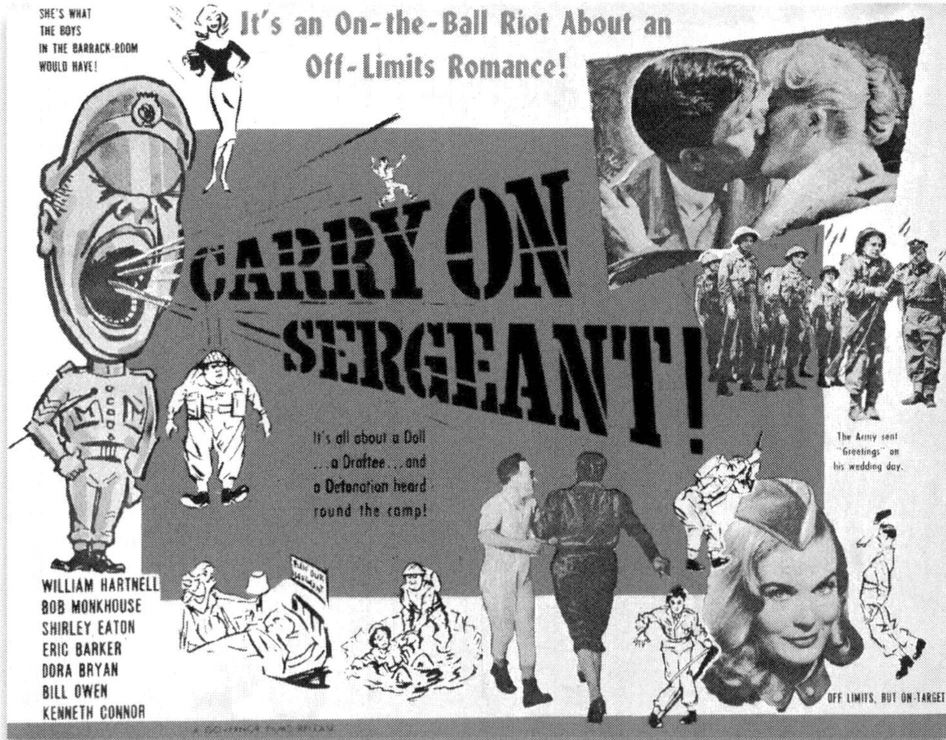

Above: *Carry On Sergeant* has more in common with the gentle British comedies of the late 1950s, but it introduced many of the initial repertory company that appeared in the Hudis-era films.

Below: Shirley Eaton and Terence Longdon in *Carry On Nurse*, a surprise hit in the USA.

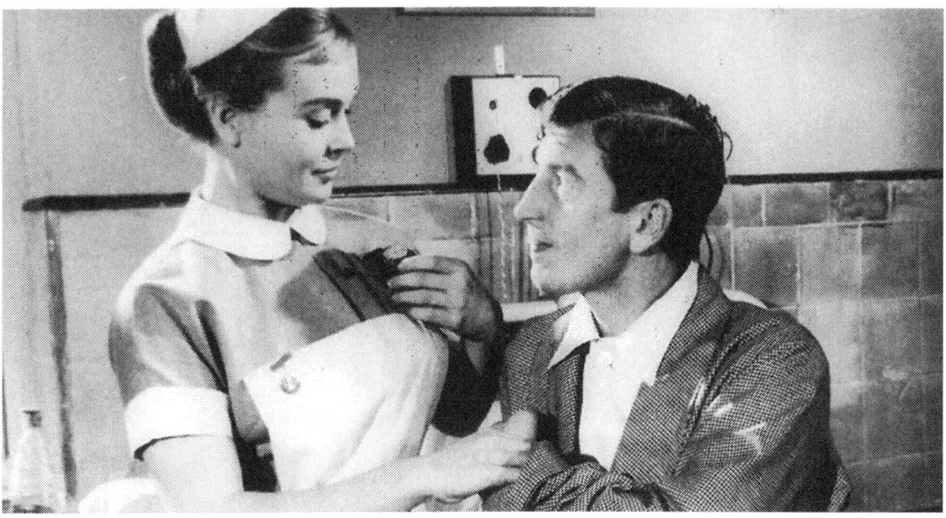

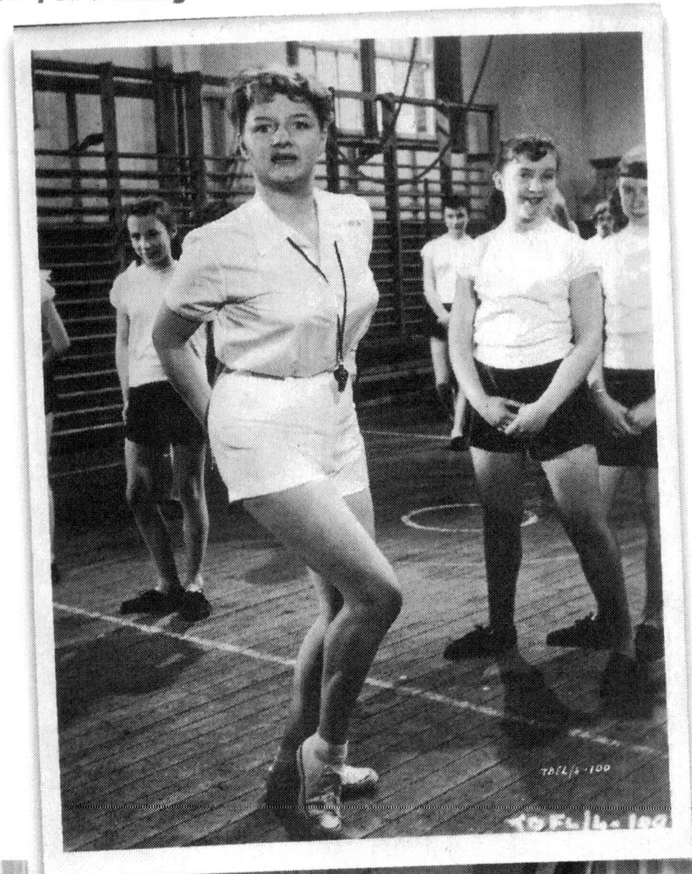

Left: Joan Sims takes a gym class in *Carry On Teacher,* which also featured Ted Ray and a young Richard O'Sullivan.

Below: The regular cast was starting to establish itself by *Carry On Constable,* which also marked Sid James' first appearance in the series.

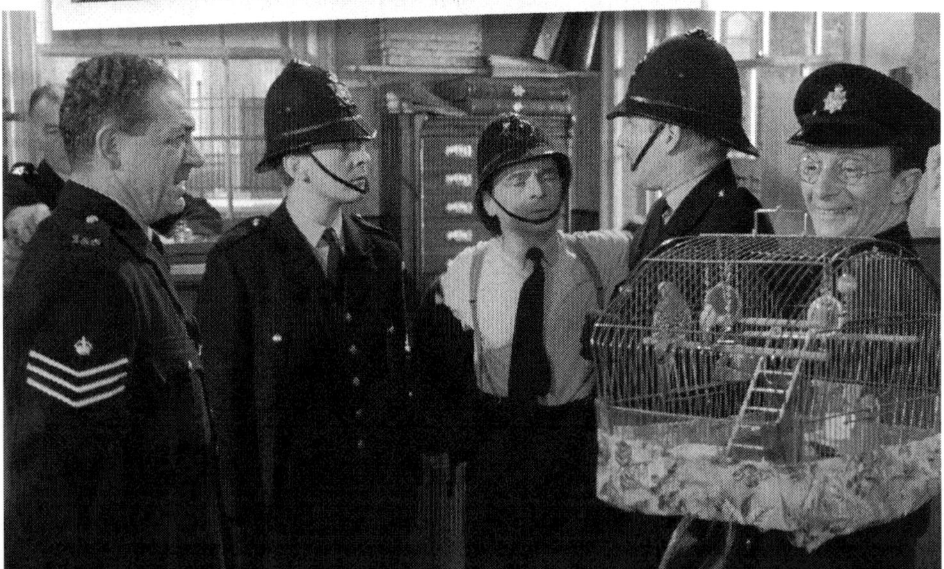

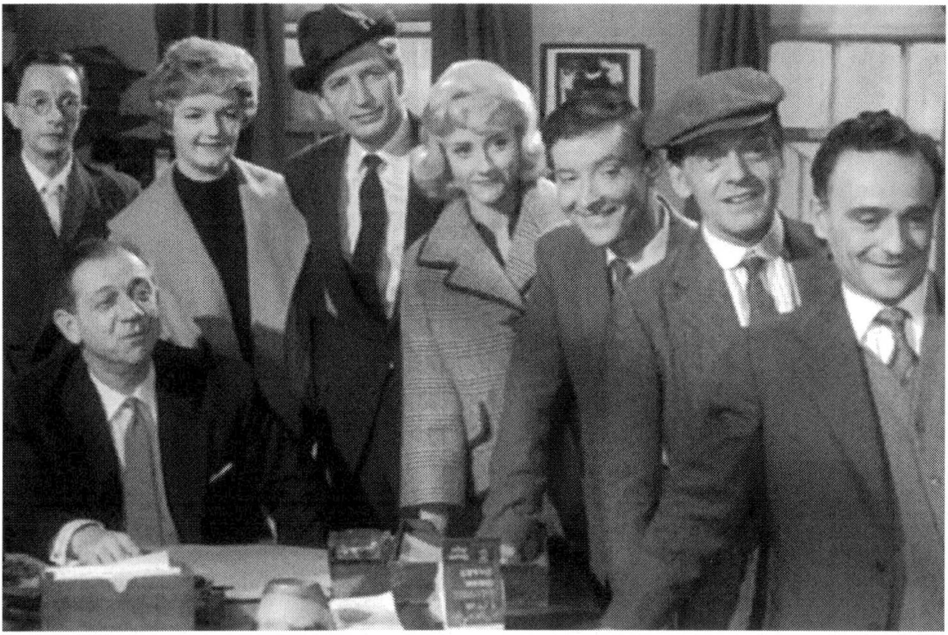

Above: The episodic *Carry On Regardless* featured semi-regular Bill Owen, second from the right, and a bizarre guest appearance from Stanley Unwin.

Below: Kenneths Williams and Connor in *Carry On Cruising*, the first of the series to be made in colour, and the last of the Hudis era.

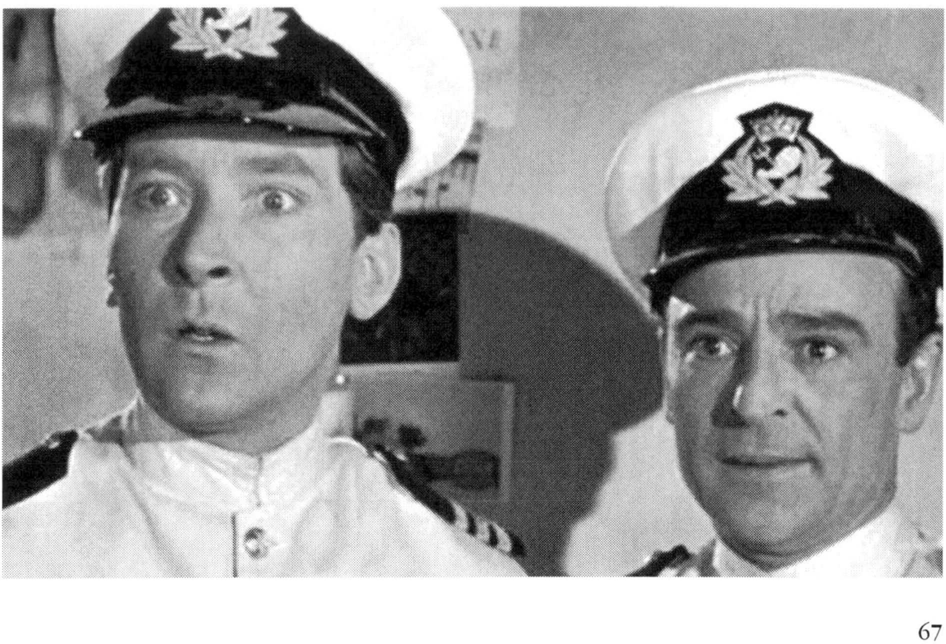

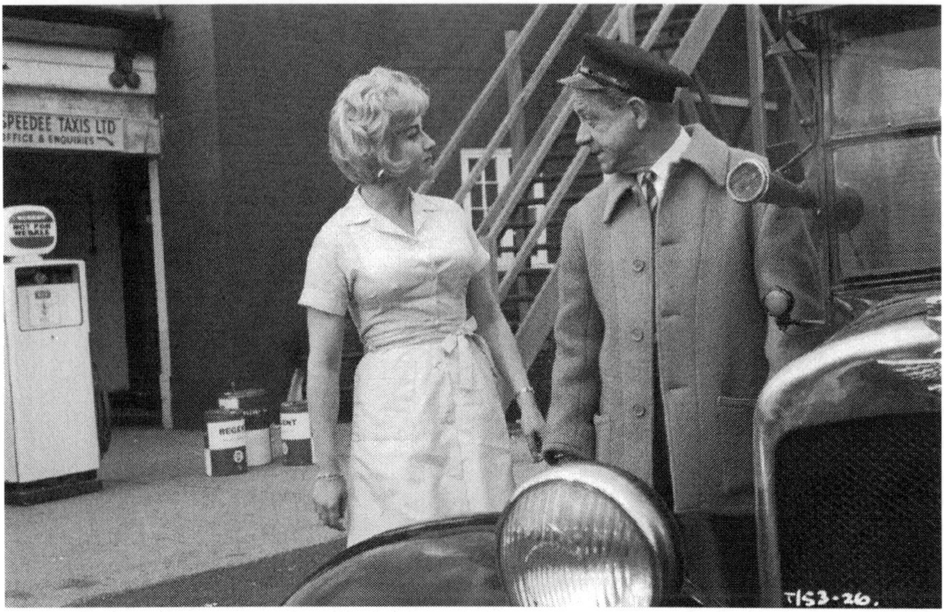

Above: Liz Frazer and Sid James in *Carry On Cabby*. Initially called *Call Me Cab*, the film was pulled into the series late in the marketing process.

Below: Guest players Juliet Mills and Bernard Cribbins alongside Kenneth Williams in *Carry On Jack*.

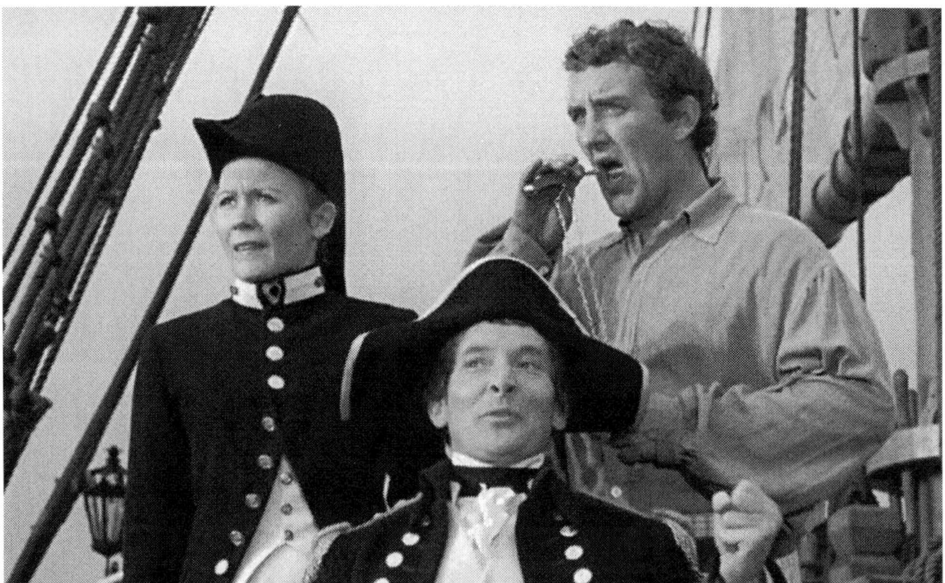

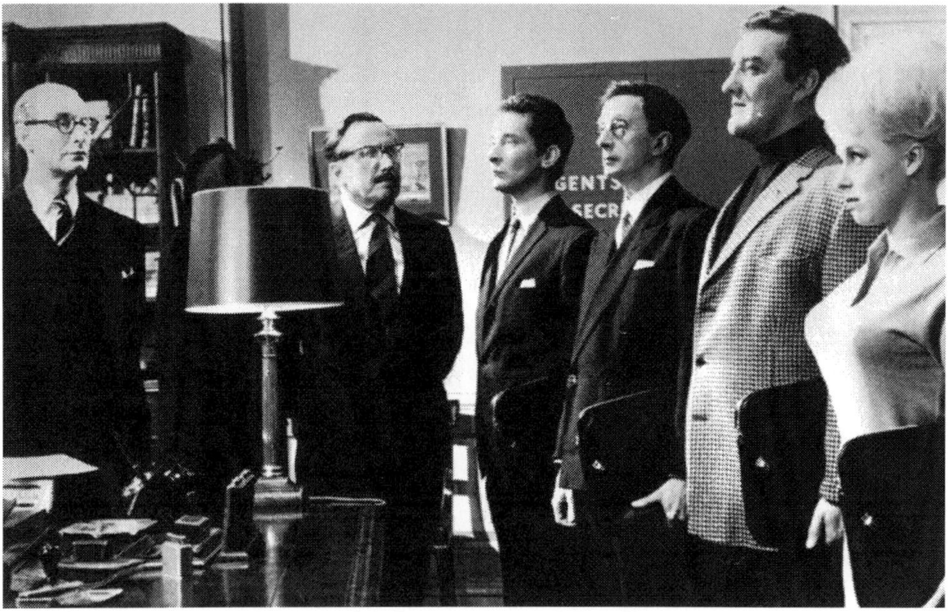

Above: Cribbins was back for *Carry On Spying* alongside Barbara Windsor making her series debut, plus vereran performers Richard Wattis and Eric Barker.

Below: *Spying* was good, but *Carry On Cleo*, starring Amanda Barrie, was a classic.

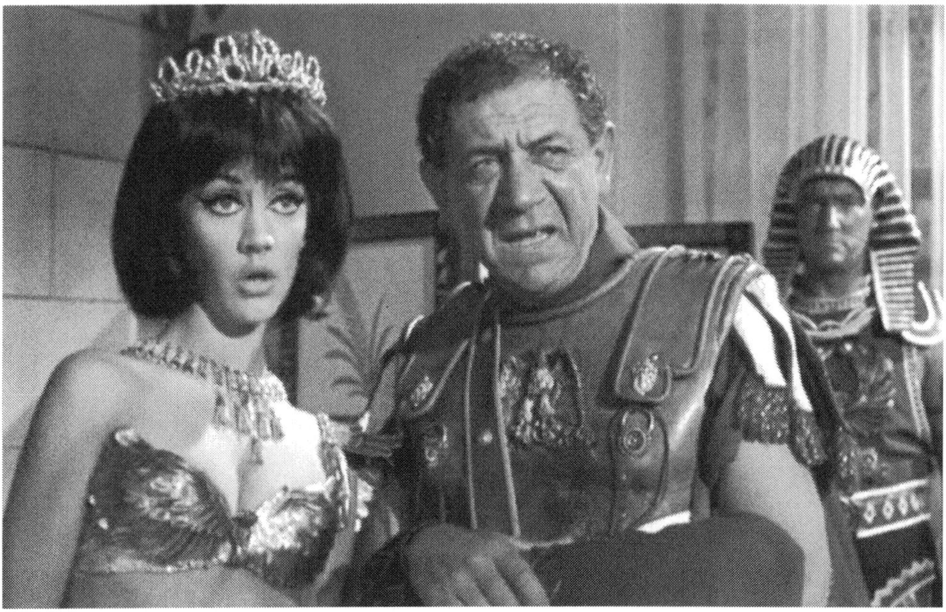

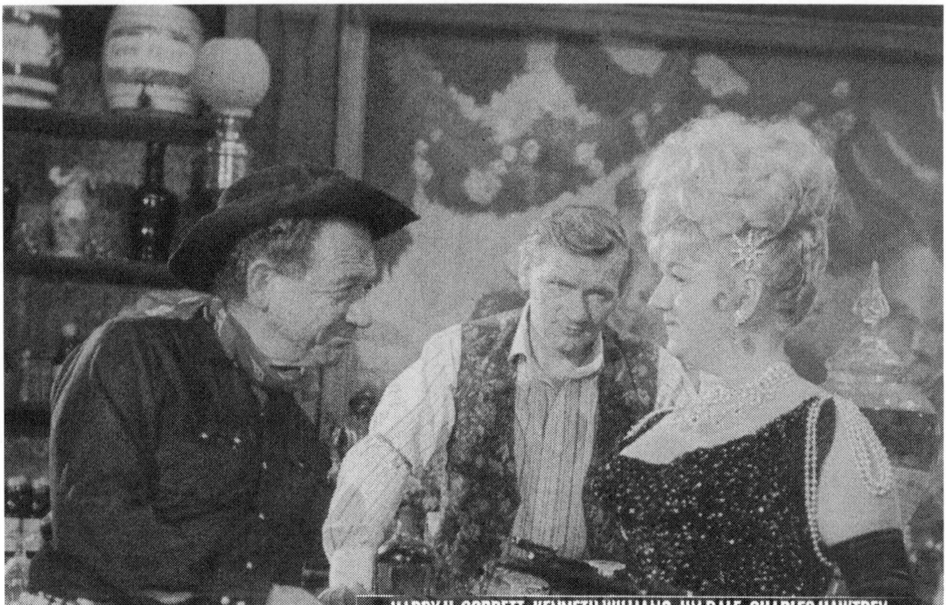

Above: Continuing the sequence of high-quality series outings, *Cowboy* is this author's favourite *Carry On,* and features Jim Dale's first romantic lead.

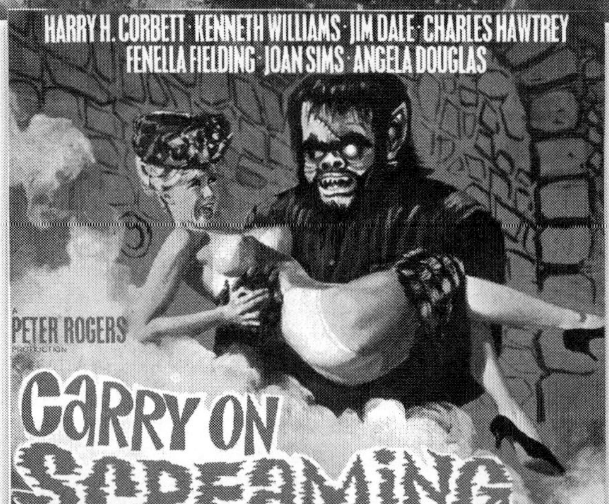

Right: 'Frying Tonight'! *Carry On Screaming* featured Harry H. Corbett in a role written originally for Sid James, and a perfectly-cast Fenella Fielding.

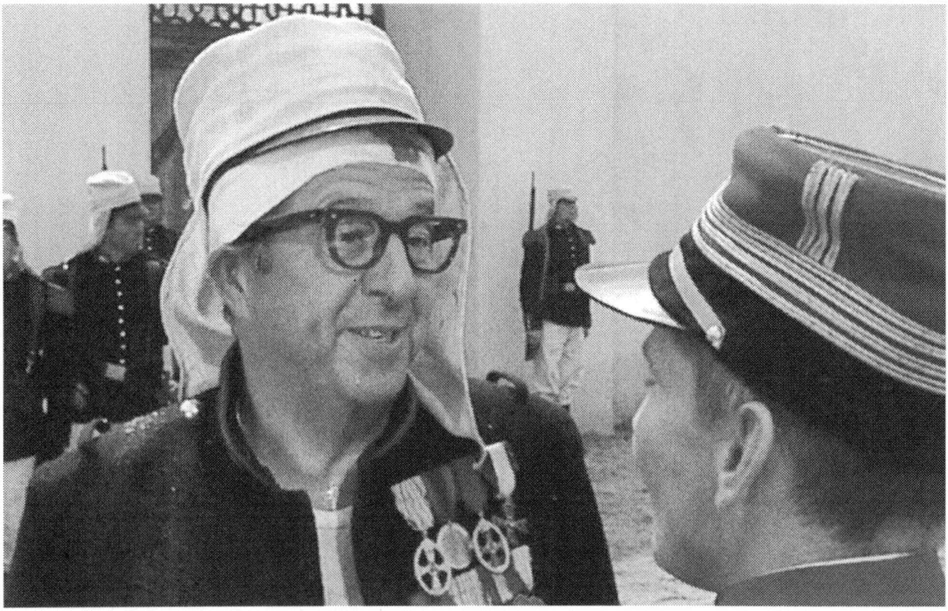

Above: *Carry On Follow That Camel* starred guest Phil Silvers, who was paid a relative fortune for his appearance.

Below: Like the film before it, *Carry On Don't Lose Your Head* became part of the series retrospectively, due to nervousness over using the series name following its move from Anglo Amalgamated to Rank.

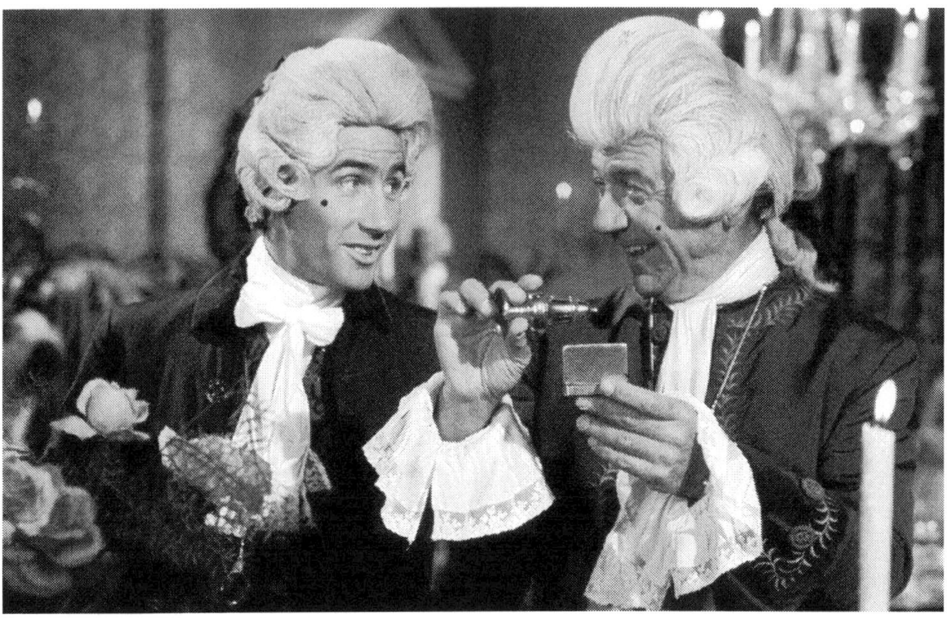

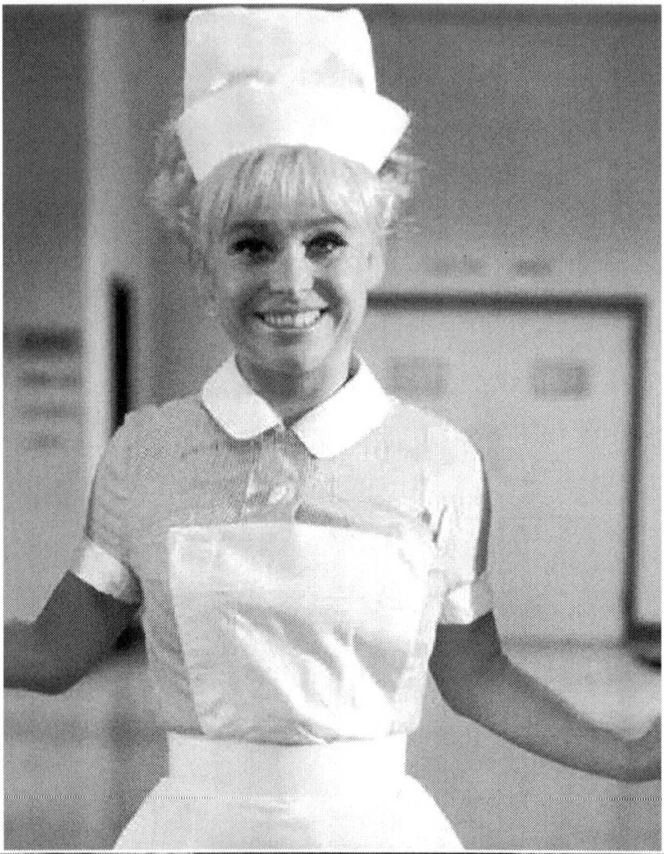

Left: Making only her second appearance in the series, Barbara Windsor shone in the excellent *Carry On Doctor*, which also starred guest Frankie Howerd.

Below: Another classic, *Carry On Up The Khyber* features the famous dinner scene, made hilarious by the reactions of Peter Butterworth.

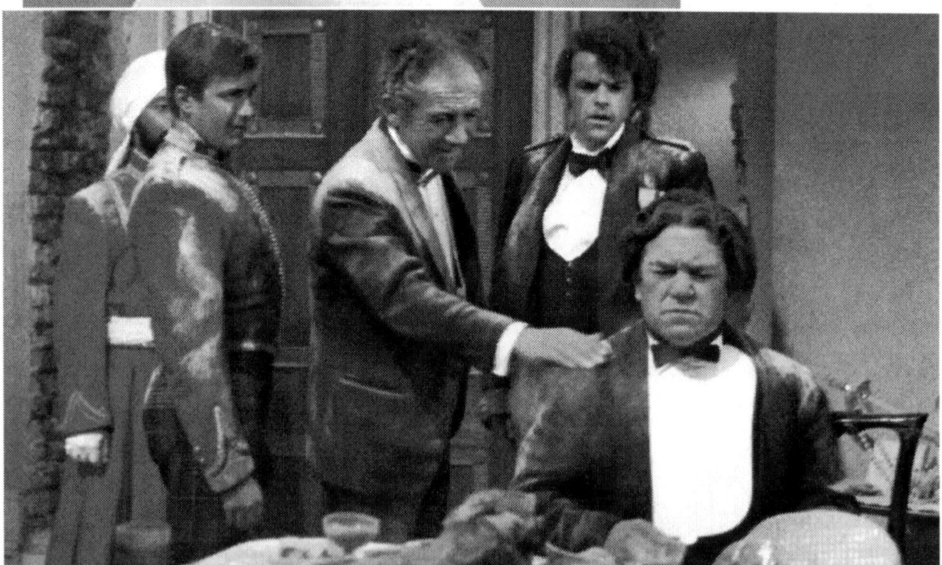

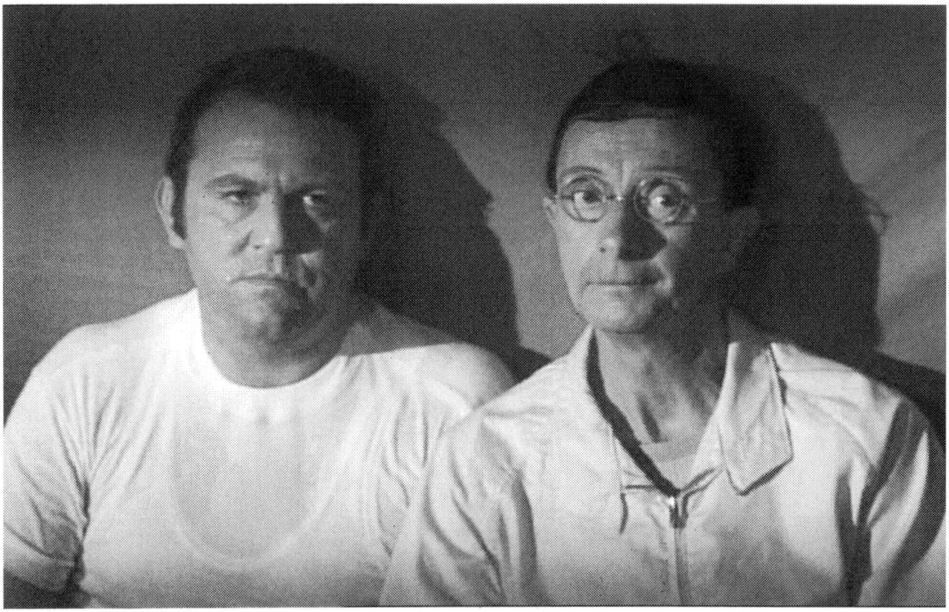

Above: *Carry On Camping* was the most successful film of any sort at the British box office in 1969.

Below: Peter Butterworth makes the best of his one-scene cameo in *Carry On Doctor Again*.

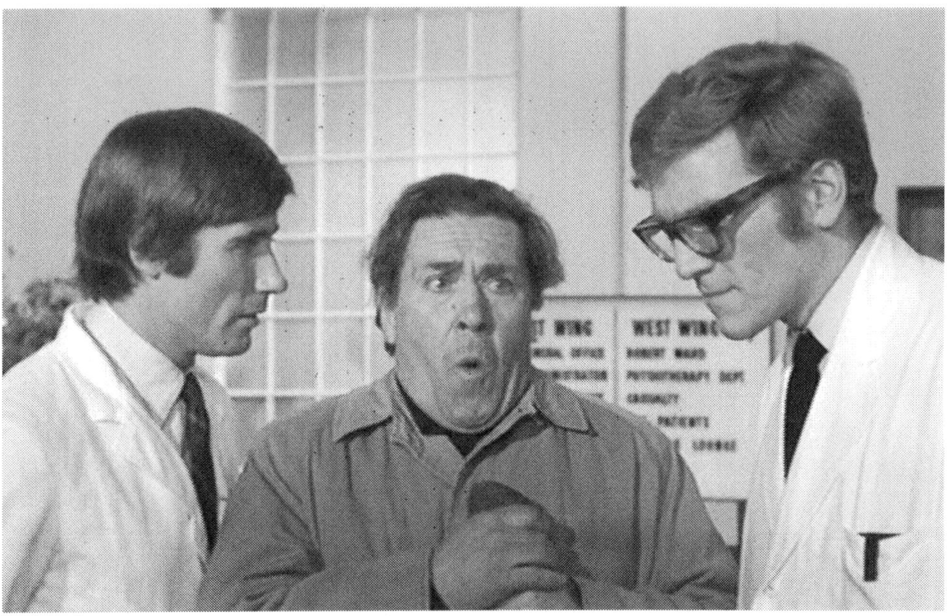

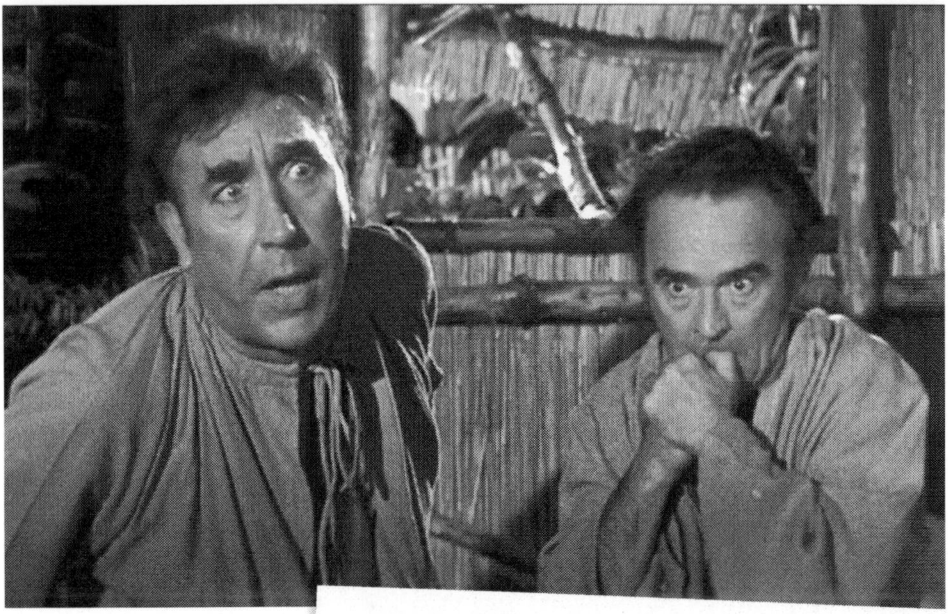

Above: *Carry On Up The Jungle* saw another appearance by Frankie Howerd and the welcome return of Kenneth Connor.

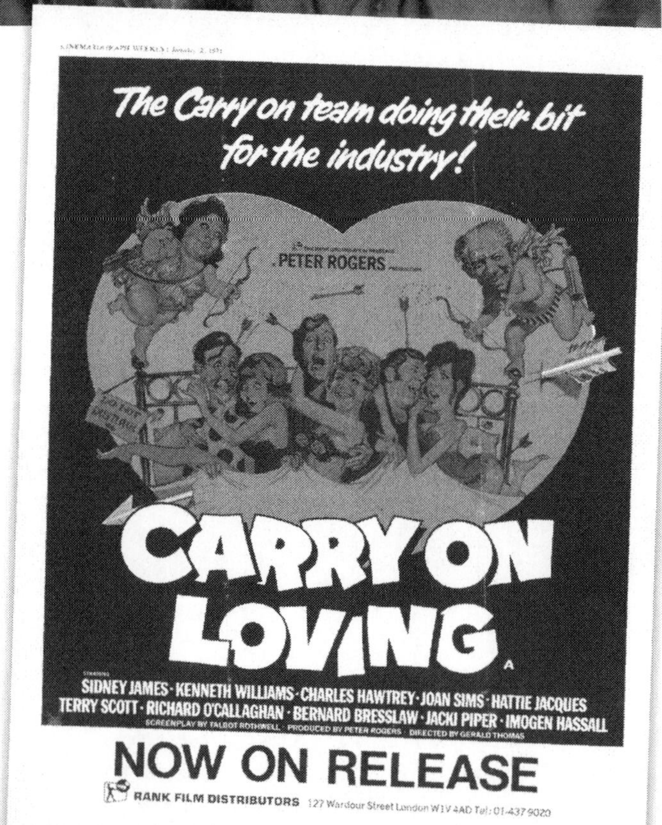

Right: *Carry On Loving* saw the series tackle the permissive age, with mixed results.

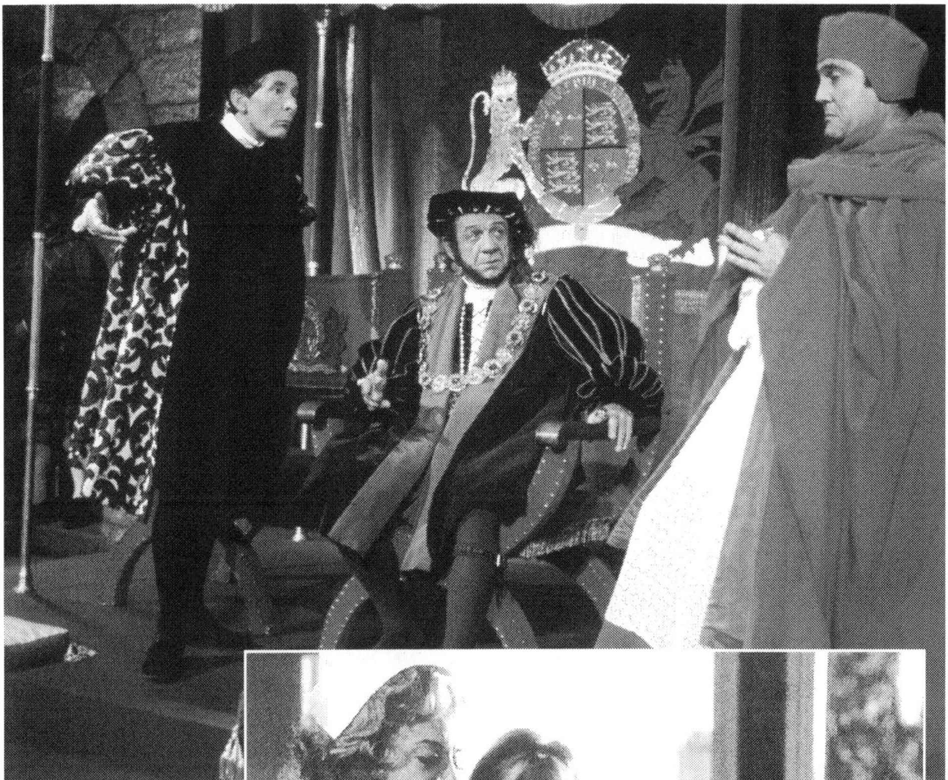

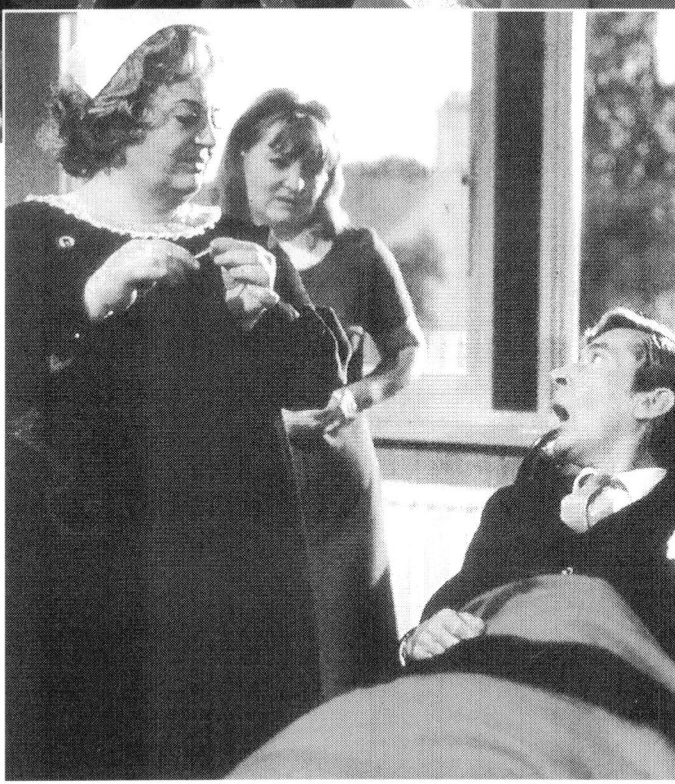

Above: The sumptuous *Carry On Henry* looked wonderful, but suffered from a somewhat tired script.

Right: *Carry On Matron* had its moments, but began to retread old ground.

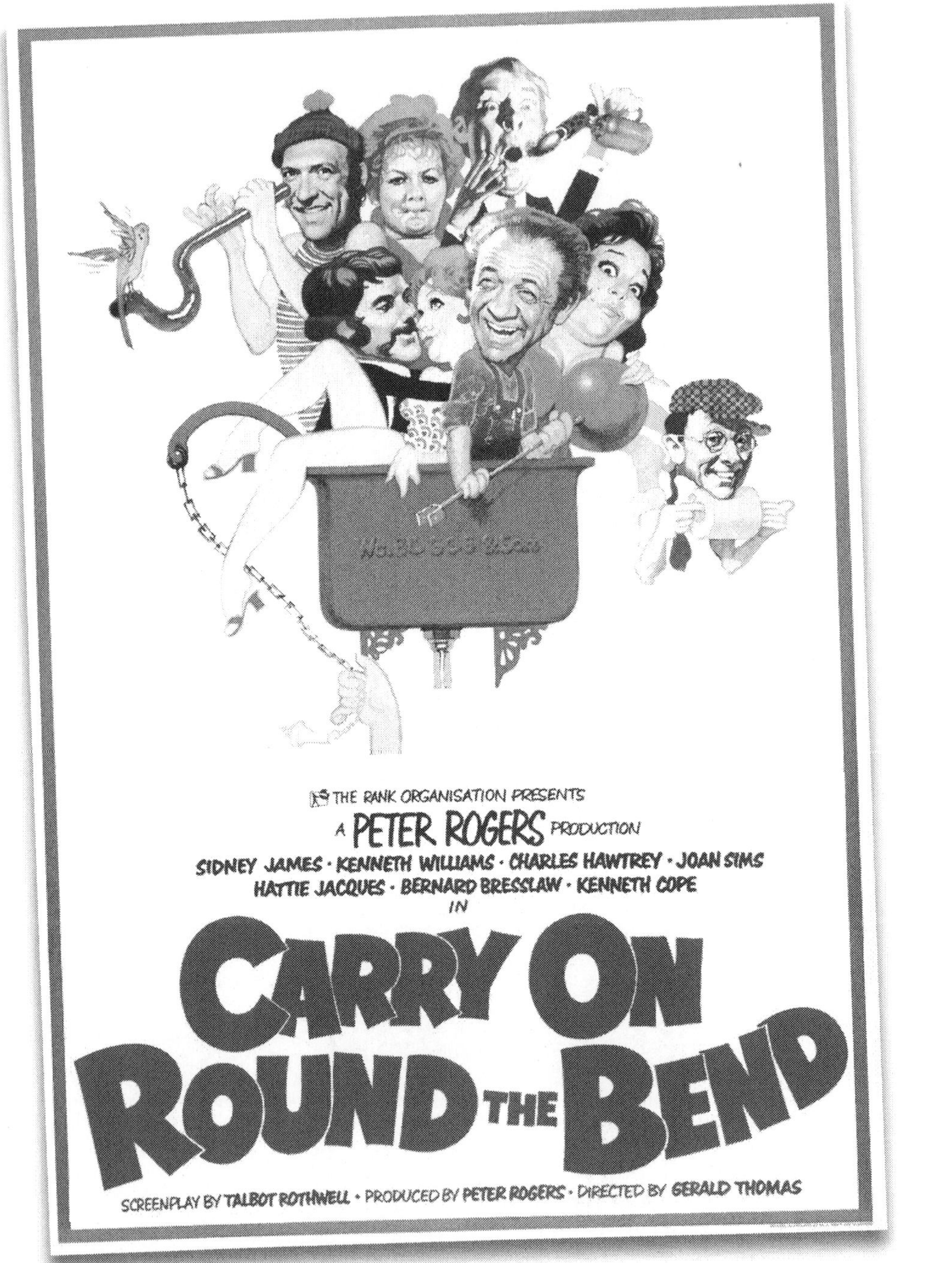

Above: *Carry On At Your Convenience* had a different title until very late in the day. It's not bad, but was criticised for some reactionary attitudes towards labour relations.

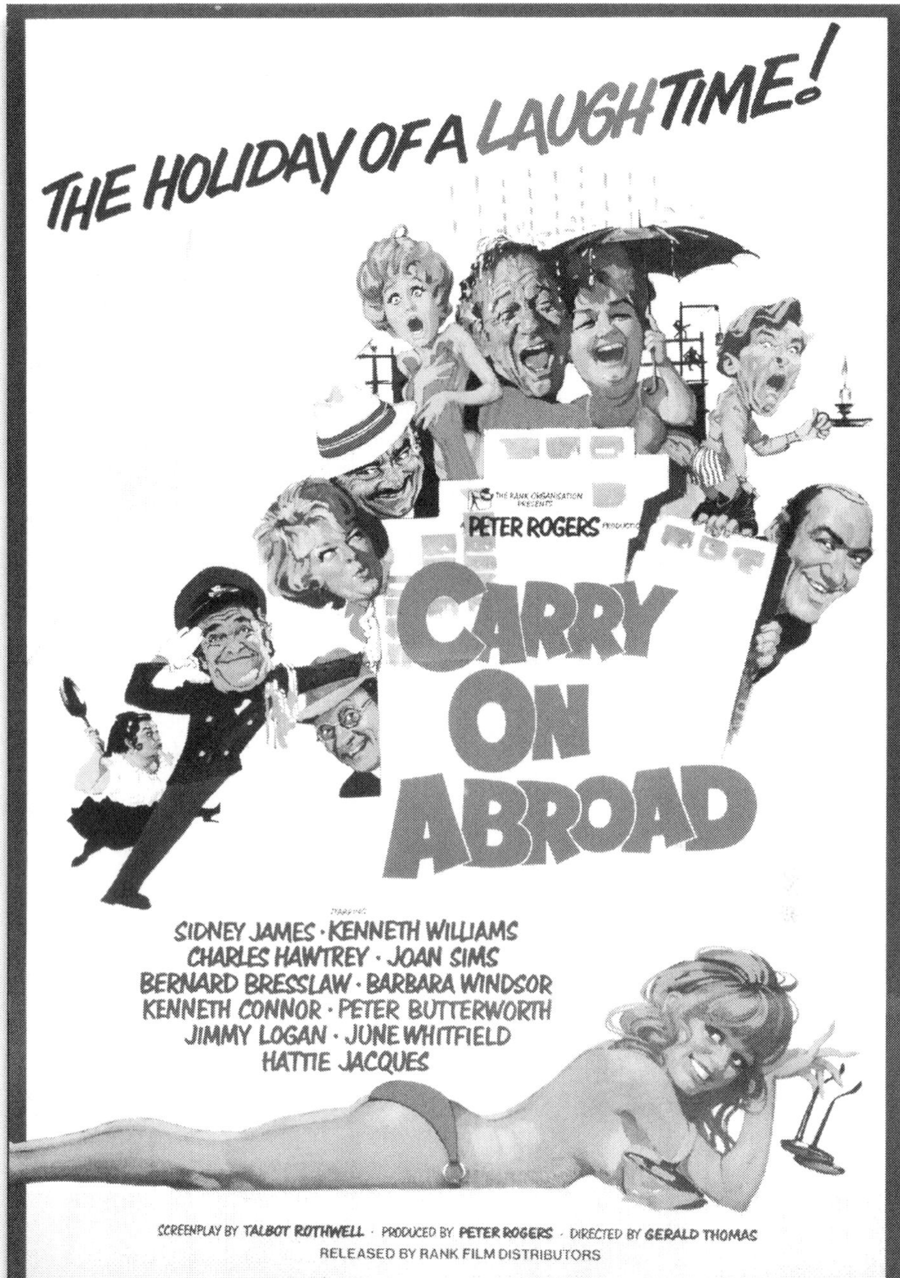

Above: *Carry On Abroad* is perhaps the last classic entry in the series, despite being filmed at Pinewood rather than in Spain as some cast members hoped. It was also Charles Hawtrey's last *Carry On*.

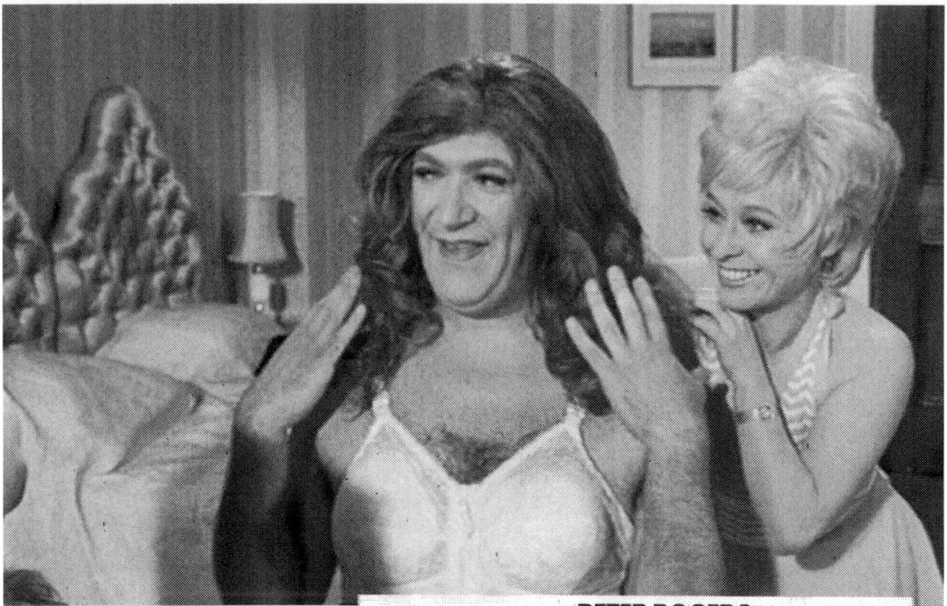

Above: *Carry On Girls* has its moments, especially a great performance from Patsy Rowlands, a regular in the 1970s films. Bernard Bresslaw in drag was less convincing, however.

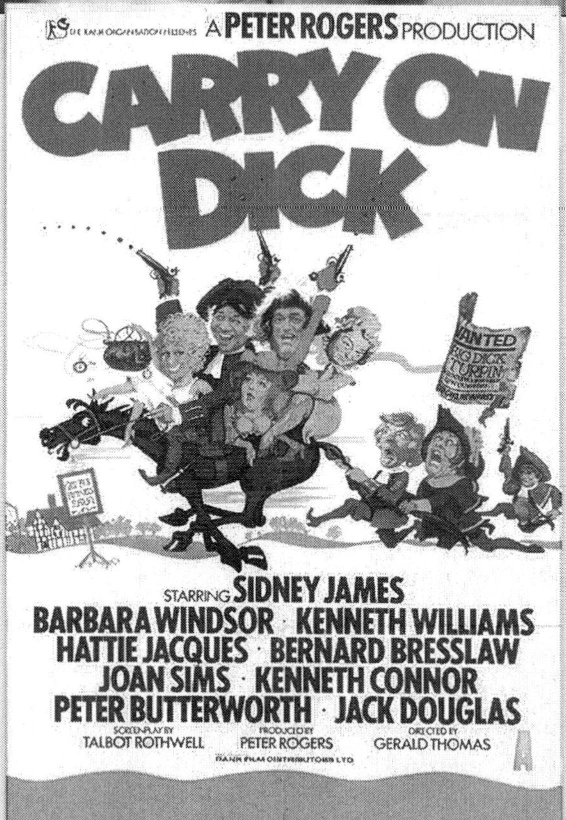

Right: *Carry On Dick* was Sid James' last appearance in a tired performance of an equally tired script.

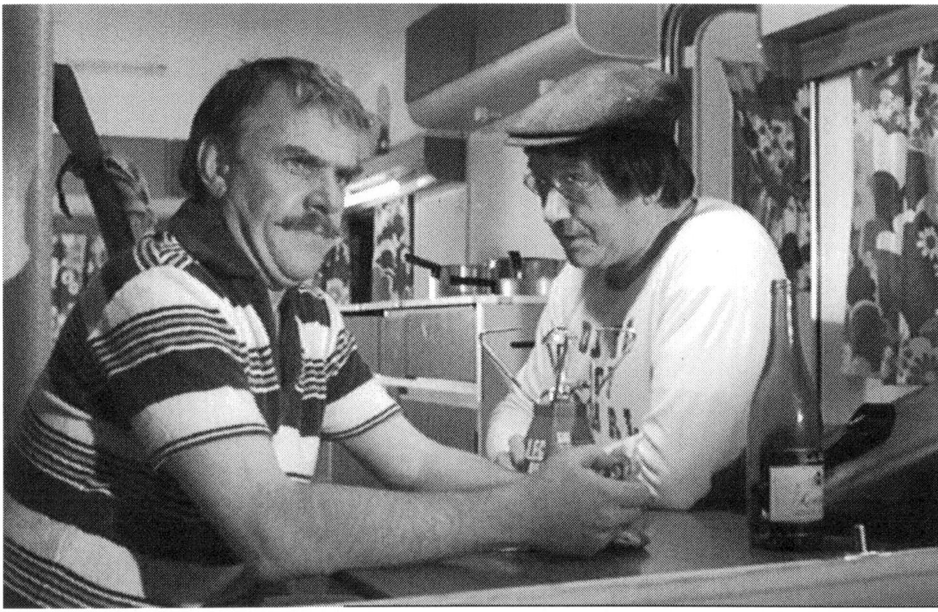

Above: Windsor Davies took over from Sid as the likeable chancer with sidekick Jack Douglas in the Dave Freeman-penned *Carry On Behind.*

Below: Davies' sergeant major schtick didn't help improve the largely forgettable *Carry On England.*

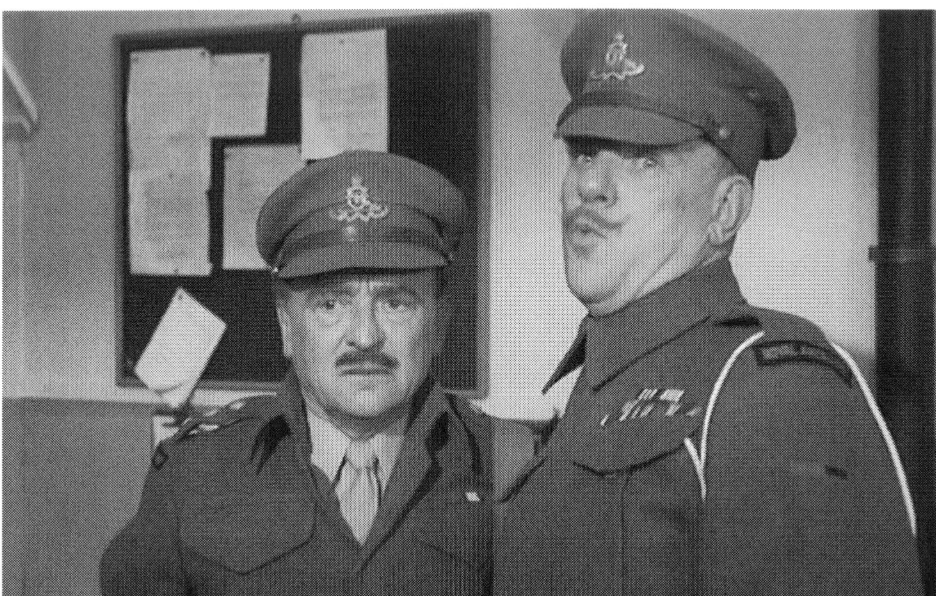

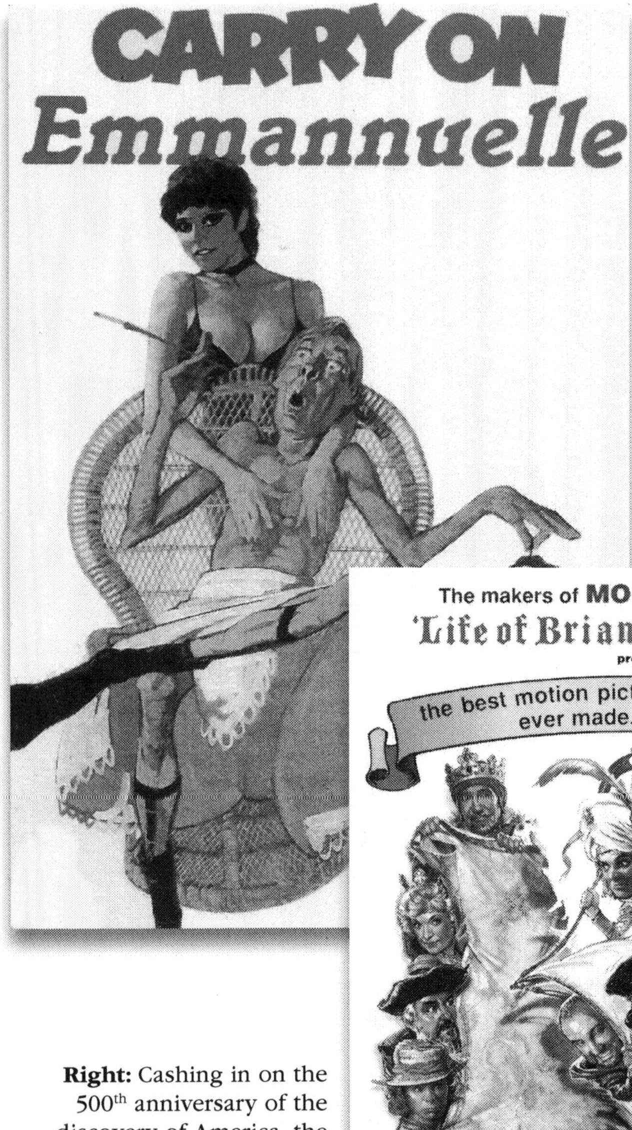

Left: Although most of the remaining regulars gave dignified performances, the same cannot be said for Kenneth Williams, who was frankly humiliated by the terrible *Carry On Emmannuelle.*

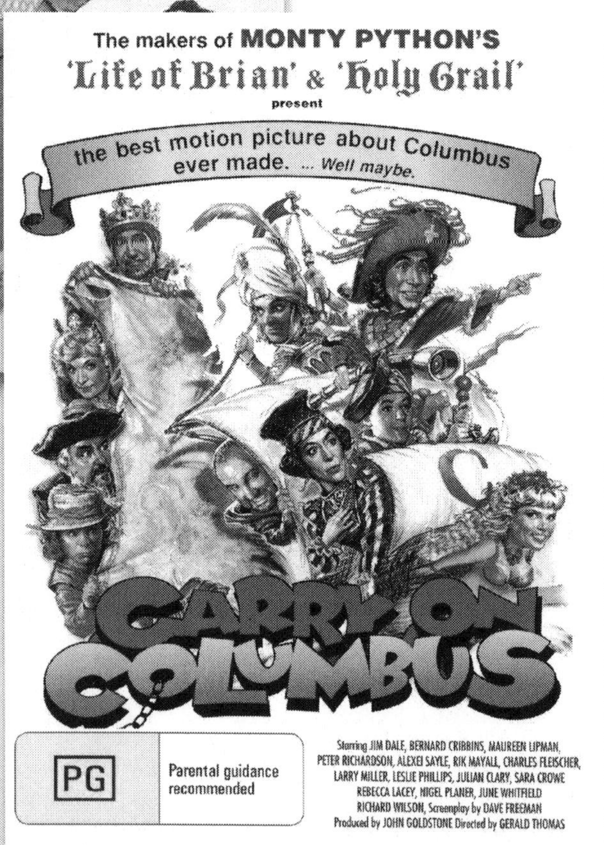

Right: Cashing in on the 500th anniversary of the discovery of America, the misconceived *Carry On Columbus* featured a host of stars from 1990s comedy alongside a somewhat bewildered Jim Dale.

Carry On ... Follow That Camel (1967)

Distributed by Rank
Produced by Peter Rogers
Directed by Gerald Thomas
Screenplay by Talbot Rothwell
Director of Photography: Alan Hume
Music composed and conducted by Eric Rogers
Filming dates: 1 May 1967 – 23 June 1967
UK release: 14 December 1967, US release: 16 October 1968
Running time: 95 minutes
Budget: £288,366

Cast:
Regulars: Kenneth Williams, Jim Dale, Joan Sims, Peter Butterworth, Charles Hawtrey, Bernard Bresslaw
Regular supporting cast: Angela Douglas, Peter Gilmore, Julian Holloway, Michael Nightingale, Sally Douglas
Guests: Phil Silvers, Anita Harris, John Bluthal, William Mervyn, Julian Orchard

Background

If Harry. H Corbett was felt to have unbalanced *Screaming,* the scales were well and truly tipped over with the casting of American star Phil Silvers as Sgt. Nocker of the French Foreign Legion in *Follow That Camel*. Silvers was famous throughout the English-speaking world as Sgt. Bilko, the star of *The Phil Silvers Show,* which ran from 1955 to 1959. Though hardly a has been, Bilko was eight years behind him, so the £30,000 payday was very welcome to the actor, as was the comfort of playing a character as close to Bilko as it was possible to be. The part had originally been earmarked for Sid James – for whom it was well suited – but Rothwell pushed for Silvers and James seems to have been ousted, although scheduling conflicts were the official line at the time. Ironically, Sid had a heart attack two weeks into the shooting schedule, so would have had to have been replaced anyway. The casting of a big star like Silvers also pleased Rank, although it seems not to have been a pleasant experience for the man himself or his co-stars, Kenneth Williams commenting on Silvers' vulgarity in his diaries. An interview with an uncomfortable-looking Silvers is available on the box set DVD – filmed on location at Camber Sands in Sussex, where the cast spent a whopping three weeks on location – and in it, he exudes insecurity. Rumour has it that the part was also offered to Woody Allen, which might also have been interesting casting, but in reality, it should have been Sid's.

The Plot

- England 1906. Falsely accused of tripping his best friend (Peter Gilmore) in a cricket match, disgraced Bertram 'Bo' West (Jim Dale) runs away to join the French Foreign Legion, only for the error to be discovered almost immediately, causing Lady Jane (Angela Douglas) – his fiancée – to follow.

- On arrival, he meets the lazy, deceiving Sgt. Nocker (Phil Silvers).
- At the Legionnaires' fort, trouble – via the local Arab tribe the Riffs – is brewing. Simpson and Bertram join up together. Nocker returns from 'patrol' feigning injury, and discovering the aristocratic behaviour of the two newcomers he reprimands them.
- After injuring the Commandant, the two are buried in sand, but realise that they can blackmail Nocker, so they escape their fate.
- Nocker starts to treat them well, even stealing the Commandant's bath. At a local club, Nocker, Bo, and Simpson meet sexy dancer Corktip (Anita Harris), despite the jealousy of Zig-Zig (Joan Sims).
- Both Nocker and Bo have encounters with Corktip, and she invites them to see her later. Meanwhile, Jane arrives at the club and is befriended by Sheikh Abdul (Bernard Bresslaw), who gets her drunk.
- Enticed by Corktip, Nocker and Bo are both captured by Abdul and taken to the Sheikh's camp, but are tracked by Simpson. Escaping, they find Jane in the camp, still two sheets to the wind.
- Bo and Simpson are captured again, but Nocker escapes. Zig-Zig tells the Commandant about Nocker's real activities while pretending to be on patrol. Nocker returns, reporting Abdul's plan to invade Fort Zuassantneuf, but is not believed until he gives more detail.
- The troop set out for Abdul's camp, but it is deserted except for Bo and Simpson who have been left for dead, and the oasis is dry.
- They set out for the Fort, short on water, finally arriving to find it ransacked and its soldiers murdered. They find Abdul's camp and Lady Jane, leaving Simpson in her place, who himself manages to escape.
- The fort is besieged, the Legionnaires improvising defence until saved by Le Pice and some reinforcements. The Commandment is killed.
- Later, back in England, Nocker – with Corktip in tow – visits Bo and Jane, who have just had a child (who looks like the Commandment).

Analysis

Even though it is far from a disaster, for me, this film is problematic. One issue, of course, is the casting of Silvers, who has a great deal of screen time. It is hard to blame the man himself, though, as the problem is in his initial casting, not his performance, which seems to me to be decent enough in the circumstances. The issue is that we have seen his shtick before, and Rothwell's dialogue for him is not quite snappy enough, despite some good lines. There are other issues, too. Rothwell's script is not up to his usual standard generally, although there are still plenty of nice touches. Kenneth Williams –as the German Commandant – seems slightly miscast, his normal exuberance somewhat constrained by his accent and haircut, though his nostrils flare impressively throughout. Worse still, Charles Hawtrey seems shoehorned into the film, his character Captain Le Pice a long way from his stock in trade, 'fey idiot'. Joan Sims, too, has an unforgiving part, though as usual she copes beautifully with an unfortunate wig.

However, Jim Dale as the heroic yet entitled Bertram and Peter Butterworth as his batman, Simpson, are both in splendid form. Butterworth must have enjoyed playing a less idiotic character for a change. Dale's physicality is once again hugely impressive. It is clearly him – not a stuntman – that falls off the camel onto his head. However, his sexual naivety is also charming, and his scene with Corktip is hilarious. Bernard Bresslaw is also superb, giving a terrific, terrifying performance as Sheikh Abdul, played dead straight. Angela Douglas is sweet as ever in her penultimate Carry On, but the real revelation here is Anita Harris as the treacherous Corktip. For those of us who think of her as a family entertainer and singer, her belly dance is something of a surprise, to put it mildly. She was to play a more typically sweet character in *Doctor* the following year.

However, *Follow That Camel* has not aged as well as many of the other films in the series. Some scenes – especially the running joke where Angela Douglas' Lady Jane is repeatedly exploited sexually as she travels to find Bertram – do not feel comfortable today. Nor does the casual racism with which the 'blacked up' Arab characters are portrayed, despite the brilliance of Bresslaw's performance.

Incidentally, the Bresslaw / Douglas storyline, which seems her almost willingly submit to becoming a member of his harem, recalls the 1921 Rudolph Valentino vehicle *The Sheikh*, an interesting touch. Most significantly, the film gets bogged down in its middle third, with the Legionnaires spending far too much time staggering around in the desert (actually Camber Sands in Sussex) to little purpose. Jokes about building sandcastles and mirages fall unusually flat.

Some readers may feel that I am being too harsh on the film yet during a period when the very highest standards were being set by the team, this is one film that fails to hit the mark.

Carry On Doctor (1967)

Distributed by Rank
Produced by Peter Rogers
Directed by Gerald Thomas
Screenplay by Talbot Rothwell
Director of Photography: Alan Hume
Music composed and conducted by Eric Rogers
Filming dates: 11 September 1967 – 20 October 1967
UK Release: 15 December 1967
Running time: 94 minutes
Budget: £214,000

Cast:
Regulars: Sid James, Kenneth Williams, Joan Sims, Peter Butterworth, Charles Hawtrey, Bernard Bresslaw, Jim Dale, Barbara Windsor, Hattie Jacques
Regular supporting cast: Peter Gilmore, Julian Holloway, Dilys Laye, Marianne Stone, Valerie Van Ost, Julian Orchard, Alexandra Dane, Gertan Klauber, Lucy Griffiths
Guests: Frankie Howerd, June Jago, Derek Francis, Dandy Nicholls, Peter Jones, Derek Guyler, Gwendolyn Watts, Harry Locke, Brian Wilde, Pat Coombs, Gordon Rollings, Patrick Allen

The Plot

- Francis Bigger (Frankie Howerd), who makes a living as an alternative practitioner, tells his audience that Doctors are unnecessary. However, he winds up in hospital after hurting his back.
- Before moving to a private room he meets his fellow patients: Charlie Roper (Sid James), a malingerer, trying to stay in hospital for as long as possible; Mr. Barron (Charles Hawtrey), suffering from a phantom pregnancy; Ken Biddle (Bernard Bresslaw), recovering from an appendix operation and enamoured of Mavis (Dilys Laye) in a ladies ward; Mr. Smith (Peter Butterworth), sore after a hernia operation. We also meet junior Doctor Kilmore (Jim Dale) who is adored by Nurse Clarke (Anita Harris) and liked by the patients. His boss is the more senior Dr. Tinkle (Kenneth Williams) who is vain and conceited yet adored by Matron (Hattie Jacques).
- Bigger misunderstands a conversation and thinks that he will die in one week, agreeing to marry his long-suffering assistant Chloe (Joan Sims).
- Meanwhile, Nurse May (Barbara Windsor) – also in love with Tinkle – arrives as a trainee, much to Tinkle's discomfort. It is implied that he may have exploited her sexually in the past when she was a patient of his, so her presence is less than welcome. His bad mood brings about a reign of terror on the patients, who all suffer various indignities.
- Tinkle rejects Nurse May, and the following day, Kilmore spots Nurse May sunbathing, mistaking it for a suicide attempt. His rescue attempt ends in

disaster. Tinkle denies any issues with Nurse May, and Matron covers for him.

- Kilmore resigns, and Nurse May leaves. The patients revolt, forcing Tinkle and Matron to confess. Tinkle is demoted, and Kilmore reinstated. Bigger finds out he is not dying and deliberately injures himself to get back into the hospital and escape Chloe.

Analysis

As *Carry On Doctor* went into production, all was not well behind the scenes. Rank was still nervous about using the moniker Carry On and with Anglo Amalgamated threatening to use the series name themselves, Rogers felt that it might be time to stop the series for good. With *Carry On Nurse* still fondly remembered and the tenth anniversary of the series looming, the last hurrah was to be a return to a modern day hospital, which might in turn allow a final tribute to the *Doctor* series of films, too, with James Robertson Justice's portrait on display in the hospital foyer. Initially planned as *Carry On Again Nurse* – or something similar – Rothwell's script demanded a change in the title, as the action was based rather more around two characters: Jim Dale's Doctor Kilmore and Kenneth Williams' Doctor Tinkle, with the two main Nurses – Anita Harris' Nurse Clarke and Barbara Windsor's Nurse May very much supporting characters. Indeed, after the denouement, when Kilmore has been reinstated and promoted, Nurse May is never referred to again.

Casting issues also produced some problems. Both Peter Rogers and Kenneth Williams were wary of yet another 'camp' actor in the cast, in Frankie Howerd, particularly as their roles were seemingly interchangeable. Indeed, had Sid James been fully fit, he might also have played Bigger (but not Tinkle). In the end, both actors were cast in roles with similar screen time, although their storylines mean they are rarely seen together, sharing only a couple of 'examination' scenes and the final operating theatre sequence.

Most of the other regulars are patients. Sid James, recovering from his heart attack, has a diminished but telling role, which comes into its own in the climactic, operating theatre sequence, while Charles Hawtrey also has a relatively small part as a father suffering from a phantom pregnancy. Peter Butterworth again has little to do, his storyline requiring him to grimace only occasionally. However, hats off to Bernard Bresslaw for his versatility, playing the type of character for which he was to become best known – a lovable, gentle but slightly gormless man – here sandwiched between two roles as terrifying ethnic warriors. The man could act! Joan Sims is given a very different part to play with as the shy, deaf Chloe Gibson, who gets her man in the end, albeit only for a few moments. She too demonstrates her great, and rarely exploited, versatility. Hattie Jacques plays the first of her lovelorn spinsters, desperately in love with Kenneth Williams. Watch out for a brief cameo from Carry On regular Alexandra Dane as a somewhat severe anti-natal class instructor. When next seen, she would have a featured role in *Khyber* as Busti, and her Carry On career was very much built around the size of her chest. But her role in *Doctor* might have heralded a different career path. Such was the lot of women in the 1960s and 1970s.

There are plenty of nods to *Carry On Nurse*, most notably the gentle tone of some of the humour. For instance, the moment when Ken Biddle (Bernard Bresslaw) is caught trying to peek at Mavis (Dilys Laye) might have come from a Norman Hudis script. *Nurse* is also referred to when Nurse Parkin (Valerie Van Ost) attempts to give Bigger some flowers. 'No you don't,' says Bigger 'I saw that film'. Harry Locke is cast as ambulance driver Sam, following his casting – nine years earlier – as Irish orderly Mick in *Nurse*, while Marianne Stone – cast as Cyril Chamberlain's wife in *Nurse*, is cast in *Doctor* in a feature part – probably her best in the series – as a frustrated mother who has constant problems with her son getting his head stuck in a bedpan. Elsewhere, as with *Nurse*, a lot of the humour comes from visiting time, and the patient's relationships with wives and friends, albeit with a broader, Rothwell-era edge. Hattie Jacques, of course, plays a Matron for the second of four times. Most importantly, the operating theatre scene in *Nurse* is repeated in *Doctor*, albeit with a tougher moral edge.

There are also nods towards the many hospital dramas that have been ubiquitous on television for more than fifty years, but these references are not sustained, and like Nurse, this is very much an ensemble film, with various storylines running through it. Some – like Peter Butterworth's hernia pain – are little more than running jokes, while others – like Francis Bigger's story and the attempt by Tinkle to oust Kilmore- have more screen time. These two storylines give the film its backbone, allowing the subplots and jokes to work around them. They also provide the film's set pieces, with the rooftop scene allowing Jim Dale once again to show his physical ability, and once he lands in the bath, his comedic chops, too.

There are some great lines as always. Bowing under the power of Matron's seduction, Doctor Tinkle exclaims, 'I was once a weak man' to be countered by Matron with 'Once a week is enough for any man!' This is typical, classic Rothwell. The wedding scene is also hilarious, with both Peter Jones' chaplain and Joan Sims' dedicated assistant unable to hear a thing, to Howerd's frustration and the growing hilarity of the crowd accumulating outside his door. Frankie Howerd is superb in *Doctor*, demonstrating that he did not always need a studio audience to be funny.

Barbara Windsor also makes a real mark in only her second Carry On, her 'Oh, what a lovely pear' quickie with Peter Gilmore is another oft quoted and much seen moment. You have to feel for Peter Gilmore. He was a fine, versatile actor who, quite rightly, became famous for his starring role in the television drama *The Onedin Line* during the 1970s. Yet he will be forever immortalised for eating a pear and saying the words 'you took the words right out of my mouth' in a Carry On film with Barbara Windsor.

Carry On Doctor remains one of the better films of the series, not because it is the funniest, but because it has all the elements to produce great, timeless comedy. It has wit, charm, irony, good jokes and a series of storylines that coalesce beautifully at the end. Coming after the relative disappointment of *Follow That Camel,* this was another classic, and, as it turned out, not the end of the series at all.

Carry On ... Up The Khyber (1968)

Distributed by Rank
Produced by Peter Rogers
Directed by Gerald Thomas
Screenplay by Talbot Rothwell
Director of Photography: Ernest Stewart
Music composed and conducted by Eric Rogers
Filming dates: April and May 1968
UK release: 28 November 1968, US release: 12 December 1968
Running time: 88 minutes
Budget: £260,000

Cast:
Regulars: Sid James, Kenneth Williams, Joan Sims, Peter Butterworth, Charles Hawtrey, Bernard Bresslaw, Terry Scott
Regular supporting cast: Angela Douglas, Peter Gilmore, Julian Holloway, Valerie Leon, Alexandra Dane, Johnny Briggs
Guests: Roy Castle, Cardew Robinson, Wanda Ventham, Patrick Allen

The Plot

- Khalabar, 1895. There is a delicate truce between the ruling British and local nationalists, perpetuated by fear in the fierceness of the British Army. However, when Private Widdle (Charles Hawtrey) of the Khyber Pass-based Third Foot and Mouth regiment – 'the Devils in Skirts' – is discovered to be wearing underpants by warrior Bungdit Din (Bernard Bresslaw), a crisis looms.
- The Governor, Sidney Ruff-Diamond – who neglects his passionate wife – realises the importance of the incident, trying diplomatic means to solve it by visiting the Khasi (Kenneth Williams) with Captain Keene (Roy Castle) and Sergeant Major Macnutt (Terry Scott).
- Asked to show that the other soldiers in the regiment do not wear underpants, it transpires that the two men are both wearing pants too.
- Keene and the Khasi's daughter, Jeli (Angela Douglas) fall in love. The whole regiment is tested, and is all wearing underwear, which Lady Ruff-Diamond photographs and takes to the Khazi, hoping to trade the photograph for sexual favours. She decides to leave with the Khasi, who travels to the Khyber Pass to tell his soldiers of the British's fallibility.
- Jeli warns Keene of the intended uprising, and they hatch a plan to get the photo back, using a local preacher – Brother Belcher (Peter Butterworth) – as a guide. Keene, Macnutt, Belcher and Widdle infiltrate the Burpas. Entering the fortress, they are mistaken for tribal chiefs and shown hospitality.
- Their identities are revealed, and they are scheduled to die, alongside Lady Ruff-Diamond, who is warned by Jeli. The Princess hatches a plan to save

everyone by dressing as a dancing girl. They escape with the help of Fakir, a local magician (Cardew Robinson).

- They return to the Pass to find that the Regiment has been massacred. The photograph is finally revealed, and the Burpas attack again. Our heroes rush back to the residency, which comes under attack during dinner.
- The British are unconcerned except Belcher, even when the Fakir's severed head is served to them. The men once again lift their kilts, and the Burpas flee, including the Khazi.

Analysis

With *Zulu* released in 1966, Rogers once again moved quickly with his next parody, putting his take on such films into production in the middle of 1968. Although opinions differ over the relative merits of *Follow That Camel* and *Up The Khyber* there is little doubt that *Khyber* is one of the best-loved of the series. The question is, why does it succeed so well, and why has it stood the test of time?

Set at the end of Queen Victoria's reign, its subject matter is historical – the British Raj at the height of its powers – rather than literary, as with *Follow That Camel*. This is a more familiar, almost comfortable, subject for its British audience, despite ongoing re-evaluations of the merits (or lack thereof) of the British in India. With Sid James now recovered from his heart attack and in a leading role perfectly suited to him, and good parts for both Joan Sims – playing a similar 'common girl made good' character as she did in *Don't Lose Your Head* – and Charles Hawtrey – back to his hilarious best – all is well. Sharp viewers may note that it is clear that the Snowdonia scenes were shot before the Pinewood interiors, as Joan Sims' characterisation is noticeably different in the location scenes, which actually take place late in the film.

Despite this, it is interesting to note that *Khyber* is the first film to be so certain of the onscreen personas of Sid James and Joan Sims that their characters have the Christian names Sidney and Joan. There are no casting surprises even in the newer players, with a well-cast Terry Scott making his first appearance as a leading character, and a first (and only) outing for the amiable Roy Castle, filling in for an unavailable Jim Dale. Roy shows plenty of charm but less innate physicality than Dale, but he is an excellent substitute. With the part of the Fakir going to the lesser-known Cardew Robinson, as opposed to the starrier but unavailable Frankie Howerd or (rather scarily) comedian and magician Tommy Cooper, for whom the part was clearly written, there are no casting impediments to unbalance the film.

Khyber slips onto slightly more difficult territory with the casting of Kenneth Williams as the Khasi and Angela Douglas as his daughter Princess Jeli, not to mention Bernard Bresslaw – in great form once again – as another fierce, ethnic warrior. Such casting, even within an established ensemble, would not be acceptable today, and in addition, all these roles are homogenised as far as possible, with little 'blacking up', just a gentle tanning in the actor's make-up.

That said, Rothwell's script does play lip service to the complexity of the situation in the region. The Indian characters are seen as fierce, nationalistic and proud, rather than evil, even if the British triumph by the skin of their teeth in the end. Williams, in particular, is excellent, delivering the ornate dialogue and rounded vowels with relish as the Khasi trades polite jibes with Ruff Diamond in the diplomatic scenes.

When the film went into production *Doctor* had not yet been shown, so initial plans were for it to have a non-Carry On title. However, by the time it was released, the series title had been re-established. The cast and crew spent one week in the most remote location of any of the series, at the foot of Snowdon in the Llanberis Pass in North Wales, doubling as the mountainous Khyber Pass. But it is a Pinewood studio set that provides the film's most famous scene, the shelling of the Governor's residence. Fuller's Earth was used to approximate falling plaster, and Joan Sims' 'I seem to be a little plastered' line was improvised. This scene is a merciless send-up of the British stiff upper lip, made all the funnier by having one character – Peter Butterworth's Brother Belcher – that is obviously terrified and hilariously so, in what is yet another great performance from the veteran actor. Angela Douglas is hardly seen in this scene, even though she is at the table, as she was laughing so hard throughout the take that no shots of her face could be used.

Rothwell's script for *Up The Khyber* also has great fun with the concept of men in kilts. 'Always ready for action' is the motto of the Third Foot and Mouth (Rothwell may just be this country's finest exponent of the silly name), and much play is also made of the concept of 'Tiffin', which is his most obvious euphemism for sex yet.

In fact, almost every word of Indian origin in the English language has a pun based around it at some point in the film. There is even a joke at Rank's expense, involving a gong – 'rank stupidity'. However, it is the cohesive plot, which makes sense, for a change, and the excellent pace, which makes *Up The Khyber* the real success it is. One final touch has the British flag in the final shot, showing the motif 'I'm backing Britain', a reference to a short-lived (and now almost forgotten) campaign by British workers – later endorsed by Prime Minister Harold Wilson – to boost the British economy at the start of 1968. The film is another 1960s classic.

Carry On Camping (1969)

Distributed by Rank
Produced by Peter Rogers
Directed by Gerald Thomas
Screenplay by Talbot Rothwell
Director of Photography: Ernest Stewart
Music composed and conducted by Eric Rogers
Filming dates: 7 October to 22 November 1968
UK release: 30 June 1969, US release: 20 June 1969
Running time: 88 minutes
Budget: £208,354

Cast:
Regulars: Sidney James, Kenneth Williams, Joan Sims, Peter Butterworth, Charles Hawtrey, Bernard Bresslaw, Terry Scott, Barbara Windsor, Hattie Jacques
Regular supporting cast: Michael Nightingale, Dilys Laye, Julian Holloway, Derek Francis, Valerie Leon, Brian Oulton
Guests: Betty Marsden, Amelia Bayntun, Georgia Moon, Anna Karen

The Plot

- The film has three storylines that converge during the film. Two frustrated friends (Sid James and Bernard Bresslaw) try to get some action from their girlfriends (Joan Sims and Dilys Laye) by taking them to a campsite that they mistakenly believe to be a nudist haven. They mess this up very badly, but the girls still give in, in the end, anyway.
- A frustrated businessman (Scott) is railroaded by his wife (Marsden) into a camping holiday where, via a series of mishaps, (many of them featuring idiotic lone hiker Charles Hawtrey) he finds fulfilment.
- Finally, a group of girls from a boarding school go on holiday led by pompous Kenneth Williams, amorous matron Hattie Jacques and lecherous bus driver Julian Holloway. Chaos ensues.
- In the films climactic scene, the three groups gang together to stop a group of hippies organising a rock festival in the field next door on the grounds that they might stop them sleeping.

Analysis

Although *Doctor* and *Spying* had – technically – been set in contemporary times, *Carry On Camping* was the first film in the series since *Cabby* in 1963 to exist in a Britain that anyone might recognise as their own. While *Doctor* was set almost entirely on the premises of a hospital, and thus existed in an almost timeless world of post war medicine, *Camping* has scenes in suburban houses with seemingly real people living ordinary lives. But this was a changed country. The permissive society was upon Britain, as was the counterculture.

So how did Thomas, Rogers and Rothwell react to this changing world? With distrust, and no little cynicism, of course.

Carry On Camping was a massive box office hit and remains much-loved. It is not hard to see why. It has a fine script from Rothwell and some of the performances, particularly Terry Scott making a second starring appearance after *Up The Khyber* and a terrifically funny turn from Peter Butterworth, are worth the price of entry alone. However, this was the film that saw an increased emphasis on sexually based humour and smutty scenarios, rather than the charm and wit that had carried the films through most of the 1960s.

Most significantly, this is the first Carry On in which almost all the main characters' motivations stem from sexual frustration. Sid James plays the latest in a series of amoral characters, with lechery in mind. Hattie Jacques plays another frustrated spinster and Terry Scott an unappreciated husband, who finds sexual fulfilment in the hands of a much younger woman and then seduces his own wife (a thankless but funny performance by the fabulous Betty Marsden – best known for her radio comedy work) by simply being more assertive.

The final scene is telling. The hippies are seen as feckless, selfish and stupid, easily outwitted by the rest of the cast based on the fact that the festival will go on all night and keep the campers awake. Since the final scenes happen in broad daylight with everyone still up and about (if a bit randy), this seems a little harsh, as there is no attempt to negotiate. The Carry On team's first encounter with contemporary Britain produces a reaction against it.

As the film has a large cast, so many regulars are underused. Joan Sims, in particular, is given little to do in a straight part after scene-stealing character turns in Carry On *Up The Khyber* and *Carry On Doctor*. The same also applies to Dilys Laye – a fine comedic actor wasted in her 'sidekick' role. Charles Hawtrey does raise some laughs, and despite his reputation for loneliness as a person, it is hard to fault his work ethic once the cameras began to roll. Kenneth Williams, too, seems to be coasting through the film in pompous authority-figure mode with a touch of 'Snide' when a funny line needs to be delivered with venom. The film does have the first – and I think only – recurring character of the series in Hattie Jacques' Matron. In a moment of dialogue when she admits her love for Williams' character, she hints that she is the same Matron who appeared in *Carry On Doctor*.

Barbara Windsor – in only her third Carry On – brings along her 'Babs' persona fully formed, and such was the power of her brief topless moment in the bra-busting exercise scene, that it has gone down as one of the most famous moments in British cinema history, with the British sensor allowing the brief flash of her breast, although this is hardly surprising given the topless scenes at the start of the film.

Camping is a good Carry On, and it is not hard to understand its long-standing popularity. It was the number one bestselling film at the UK box office in 1969, which is astonishing to imagine in this era of U.S. franchise blockbusters. It is, however, a transitional film which takes the series' risqué humour and starts the slippery slide away from wit towards smut. While it is not hard to understand why the production team chose such a path, it marked the beginning of the end for the series.

Decline And Fall – Again Doctor To Columbus

Carry On Again Doctor (1969)

Distributed by Rank
Produced by Peter Rogers
Directed by Gerald Thomas
Screenplay by Talbot Rothwell
Director of Photography: Ernest Stewart
Music composed and conducted by Eric Rogers
Filming dates: 17 March 1969 – 2 May 1969
UK release: 5 December 1969, US release: 10 May 1970
Running time: 89 minutes
Budget: £219,000

Cast:
Regulars: Sidney James, Kenneth Williams, Joan Sims, Peter Butterworth, Charles Hawtrey, Barbara Windsor, Hattie Jacques, Jim Dale
Regular supporting cast: Patsy Rowlands, Peter Gilmore, Valerie Leon, Valerie Van Ost, Billy Cornelius, Hugh Futcher, Lucy Griffiths, Alexandra Dane
Guests: Wilfred Brambell, Patricia Hayes, Pat Coombs, Elizabeth Knight, William Mervyn, Bob Todd, Gwendolyn Watts, Yutte Stensgaard, Eric Rogers, Harry Locke

Background

Given the success of *Carry On Doctor*, it is hardly surprising to see the team returning to film exteriors at Maidenhead Town Hall once again for another medically themed outing. Not that there wasn't still concern about getting too close to the *Doctor* series, with Kenneth Williams' character particularly under scrutiny for its similarity to Lancelot Spratt. They need not have worried.

Williams' Frederick Carver is a mouse of a character, not a monster. *Carry On Again Doctor* is a solid – if unspectacular – outing in the series, but has some fabulous moments, even if it is let down by a rather uncomfortable plot which takes the action away from the hospital for the majority of the film.

The Plot

- After a series of mishaps and misunderstandings, accident-prone Doctor Nooky (Jim Dale) saves his career only by accepting a posting to a medical mission in the tropics, where he meets orderly Gladstone Screwer (Sid James) who, it transpires, has invented a cure for female obesity.
- 'Borrowing' the medicine, Nooky returns to Britain and sets up in business, funded by wealthy benefactor Joan Sims. He succeeds in his business in the end, and marries model Goldie Locks (Barbara Windsor) despite the efforts of doctors Charles Hawtrey and Kenneth Williams, not to mention a vengeful Screwer looking for a piece of the action.

Analysis

With the Series at its two-per-year production height, there is a feeling of squad rotation here; the cast is made up of many new or returning bit-part players, with only Valerie Leon returning from *Carry On Camping*. Of the regulars, however, James, Williams, Sims, Windsor (in only her fourth outing), Jacques and Butterworth (in a tiny but hilarious role) all return from the movie filmed only six months earlier. Coming off the subs bench is Patsy Rowlands in her first Carry On. Her stock character – a put-upon employee or wife who gets her revenge eventually – is established here. Peter Gilmore shows his versatility as a Doctor rather than an ambulance driver, while well-known names from television like Pat Coombs, Patricia Hayes and William Melvyn all make rare appearances. Wilfred Brambell – best known for his role in the long-running situation comedy Steptoe And Son – makes a brief appearance as a pervy old man. This is a jarring, somewhat unnecessary scene and Eric Rogers, as we have seen often, a playful and inventive composer, rather overplays his hand by ramming the 'Steptoe' theme music down our throats.

Jim Dale once again plays 'our hero' – albeit one with an eye to the main chance, and rather more confidence as a ladies' man – and Windsor is his love interest. Kenneth Williams is a pompous but lily-livered consultant, and Hattie Jacques gives her standard performance as Matron, although at least she isn't lovelorn in this film. By far the most interesting piece of casting has Charles Hawtrey in a relatively straight role for a change. Gone is his foppish, fey charm, replaced by a jealous man with a nasty streak. The actor seems less comfortable outside his normal camp persona for a while until later in the film, which requires him to dress as a woman, a typical Carry On device. Joan Sims – once again – is given little to stretch her, although in the scene where Kenneth Williams attempts to woo her for her money, she is as funny as ever in a sequence that otherwise is hardly innovative.

The film is on safest, funniest ground when it stays within the hospital walls, via a few old jokes – Pat Hayes' scene is a sequence of them – and the slapstick scenes where Jim Dale's career at the hospital spirals out of control are as expertly constructed as ever, with Dale handling his own stunts and doing himself some damage in the process, too. Indeed, these early sequences contain two of the best-remembered moments in Carry On history. The first has a delightfully funny Peter Butterworth assisting in Dale and Peter Gilmore's diagnosis game, while the other – which follows directly on from the Butterworth scene – contains Dale's famous, enthusiastic, exaggerated 'corrr' when presented with a near-naked Windsor.

After an interlude in the Beatific Islands – a very convincing studio set – which introduces an exuberant Sid James having great fun in this supporting role ('Have you ever tried to milk a gnat?'), the film reaches its weakest segment – the final third, which involves Hawtrey and Williams' attempt to infiltrate Nooky's clinic. The McGuffin here is Screwer's serum to cure obesity, and his attempt to get in on the action by adding a hair-replacement serum to the mix.

It is a rather weak ending, but overall the film is a decent – if inconsequential – outing in the series, with some priceless moments.

Carry On Up The Jungle (1970)

Distributed by Rank
Produced by Peter Rogers
Directed by Gerald Thomas
Screenplay by Talbot Rothwell
Director of Photography: Ernest Stewart
Music composed and conducted by Eric Rogers
Filming dates: 13 October 1969 – 21 November 1969
UK release: 20 March 1970, US release: unknown
Running time: 89 minutes
Budget: £210,000

Cast:
Regulars: Sidney James, Joan Sims, Charles Hawtrey, Kenneth Connor, Terry Scott, Bernard Bresslaw
Regular supporting cast: Valerie Leon, Jacki Piper
Guests: Frankie Howerd, Nina Baden-Semper, Yemi Ajibade, Reuben Martin, Edwina Carroll, Danny Daniels

The Plot

- In flashback, Professor Inigo Tinkle (Frankie Howerd) gives a lecture, telling the story of his latest bird-watching exhibition in Africa with assistant Claude Chumley (Kenneth Connor) and Lady Bagley (Joan Sims) with her assistant June (Jacki Piper).
- The expedition is led by hard-drinking hunter Bill Boosey (Sid James) and his native guide Upsidasi (Bernard Bresslaw).
- Both Tinkle and Chumley are attracted to Lady Bagley, finding evidence of the legendary Oozlum bird. Lady Bagley tells the story of the loss of her husband and baby son in the jungle some years before. The party are threatened by the Nosha tribe of cannibals and a gorilla also infiltrates their camp.
- Wandering away from the camp, June befriends a 'jungle boy' (Terry Scott) and they become lovers. On a night of misunderstandings, it is revealed that the 'jungle boy' is Cecil, Lady Bagley's lost son.
- Captured by the Noshas and about to be eaten, the group are rescued by an Amazonian tribe from Aphrodisia, led by Leda (Valerie Leon), who puts the men to work as mates for the all-female tribe, the Lubidubis, whose king is Walter Bagley (Charles Hawtrey) and whose mascot is the Oozlum bird.
- The men 'perform' poorly, but Upsidasi – who had escaped earlier – returns with some army rescuers. Cecil calls up some animal friends, who trample over the army troop.
- Realising that in the soldiers the Lubidubis now have a better stock of men, the others are allowed to escape. Back at the lecture, Tinkle uncovers the Oozlum bird – to find it has disappeared, as legend suggests it should.

Analysis

By the time *Up The Jungle* wrapped towards the end of 1969, an astonishing 16 Carry On films had either been shot or released during the 1960s. With the same Director and Producer at the helm, and largely the same group of actors and crew, this was a punishing schedule by anyone's standards, even if the shooting schedules themselves rarely breached their six-week targets. Talbot Rothwell, in particular, had reached a creative peak with his elegant scripts for *Doctor* and *Up The Khyber*. How long could it last?

Rogers had wanted to tackle the Tarzan stories for some time, but with the rights unavailable, he decided to make a more generic jungle-based story, albeit with a Tarzan-like character in the Jungle Boy, Cecil. As a result, *Carry On Up The Jungle* is not a classic Carry On film. First of all, it has a strange atmosphere, shot entirely on a soundstage at Pinewood, giving it an odd, theatrical feel. Secondly, my heart always sinks when I see a man in an unconvincing Gorilla suit, and a lot of the physical humour depends on a somewhat lengthy and improbable stretch of the imagination in this direction. Thirdly, with Jim Dale unwilling to accept as poor a role as Cecil, it went instead to an admittedly very game Terry Scott. Though funny in the part, Scott was much too old for it. Indeed, at 42, he was three years older than his mother, Joan Sims. Fourthly, Rothwell's script is a little lacklustre, bogging down in its second act as his poorer scripts tend to do, and relying on obvious gags – most of them sexual – without any real wit. Finally, although acceptable at the time, the 'blacking up' of Bernard Bresslaw's character Upsidasi really does not sit well in the 21st century.

There was some good news on the casting front, however. Kenneth Connor was back after a five-year gap, albeit in a supporting role probably written with Peter Butterworth in mind, although his first 'cwwoorrr' – a few minutes in – is a nostalgic treat, and he is very convincing as a man of pent up, repressed passions. In Jacki Piper, as the demure secretary to Lady Bagley (Joan Sims), the series found a new juvenile lead in the Angela Douglas mould, but just a touch more modern in attitude. She was to appear in three more films in the series, all set in the modern day.

The middle part of the film revolves around a somewhat torturous series of misunderstandings as both Howerd and Connor attempt to sleep with Sims and Sid James attempts to seduce Jacki Piper (out of desperation), confused by the presence of Terry Scott and a very hairy gorilla.

Up until the hour mark, the film is largely saved by solid performances from James, Howerd, Connor and Sims, particularly James, who can turn a poor line into a passable one simply with his comic timing and that trademark laugh. However, the laughs begin to come thick and fast – even as the sexual politics go down the pan – as the main characters discover the Lubidubi tribe, and the action speeds up somewhat.

Up The Jungle is far from a disaster, but does stretch itself somewhat thinly over its 90-minute running time. If you can ignore the terrible 'cannibal tribe' clichés and the unfortunate sexual politics of the final third, there is some decent material there, and the cast, as always, gives it their all. But in the 1970s, the series was to become far less consistent, and *Up The Jungle* was to be the first film to show a marked dip in quality.

Carry On Loving (1970)

Distributed by Rank
Produced by Peter Rogers
Directed by Gerald Thomas
Screenplay by Talbot Rothwell
Director of Photography: Ernest Stewart
Music composed and conducted by Eric Rogers
Filming dates: 6 April 1970 – 15 May 1970
UK release: 20 November 1970, US release: not known
Running time: 88 minutes
Budget: £215,000

Cast:
Regulars: Sidney James, Kenneth Williams, Joan Sims, Charles Hawtrey, Hattie Jacques, Terry Scott, Bernard Bresslaw, Peter Butterworth
Regular supporting cast: Jacki Piper, Julian Holloway, Richard O'Callaghan, Patsy Rowlands, Joan Hickson, Bill Maynard, Tom Clegg, Derek Francis, Alexandra Dane, Patricia Franklin, Lucy Griffiths, Amelia Bayntun
Guests: Imogen Hassall, Gordon Richardson, Anna Karen, Bill Pertwee, Ronnie Brody, Kenny Lynch, Philip Stone, Mike Grady

The Plot

- The story revolves around the customers of the Wedded Bliss marriage agency. The unmarried proprietors Sid and Sophie Bliss (Sid James and Hattie Jacques) are feuding over Sid's interest in a client, Esme Crowfoot (Joan Sims), but their relationship appears harmonious to their customers.
- Suspicious, Sophie employs James Bedsop (Charles Hawtrey), a private investigator, to track Sid's movements.
- Shy Bertrum Muffet is paired up with Esme by Sophie, but at the appointment there is a misunderstanding and he meets model Sally Martin (Jacki Piper) instead, who thinks he is a photographer.
- The agency also sets up Terence Philpott (Terry Scott) with dowdy Jenny Grub (Imogen Hassell), a meeting which does not go well.
- Meanwhile, marriage counsellor and bachelor Percival Snooper (Kenneth Williams) is advised by his superior to find a wife to make him more sympathetic to his clients, so he also visits the agency.
- Impressed by his breeding, Sophie offers herself to him as a possible wife.
- Sid visits Esme again, pretending to be suicidal, but her old boyfriend Gripper (Bernard Bresslaw) arrives just as Bertrum also turns up on the 'correct' date. Gripper beats him up.
- Jenny Grub moves into Sally's flat, getting an immediate job as a model. Sally tracks Bertrum down in hospital, and they start dating.
- Terence bumps into Jenny at the agency, and seeing her transformed into a beautiful woman, they start to date, too.

- Sid learns about Sophie's plan to marry Snooper and plans to disrupt it by sending Esme to seduce him, but Snooper's housekeeper, Miss Dempsey (Patsy Rowlands), who loves him, plans the same thing. Miss Dempsey makes her play, and Esme arrives and does the same.
- Sid tips off Gripper, but Miss Dempsey beats Gripper up when he arrives. Sophie changes her mind about marrying Snooper, and she and Sid agree to marry each other.
- Bedsop reports making Sophie angry, but they still marry.
- At the end, the couples have paired off, but how happily?

Analysis

I must admit to a soft spot for *Carry On Loving*. After dabbling in the world of the permissive society in *Camping*, the series sailed towards it under full steam with the first film to be shot in the 1970s. It conveniently tackles sex by basing the film around the world of the Bliss wedding agency, run by a feuding Sid James and Hattie Jacques. Unlike *Jungle* which started very slowly before coming to life in its final third, *Loving* has the good sense to start with some decent jokes while the modern setting gives the film an 'extended TV sitcom' sort of feel, particularly during the extended misunderstanding between Bertrum and Sally and the scene late in the film where Esme Crowfoot (Joan Sims) pretends to be in love with Snooper – played by Kenneth Williams relishing a decent supporting part.

Having created a classic final scene in *Up The Khyber* with the destruction of British residence, the team were to fall back on the same sort of tactic time and again during the 1970s, and *Loving* ends with a somewhat unsatisfactory food fight at the Bliss' wedding reception. Wanton destruction does not make a good ending unless it is handled with wit, and here the action, with cream everywhere, is hurried and not particularly funny, although Sid James pouring ice down Hattie Jacques's top is a sight to behold.

The film does have plenty of good moments, though. Richard O'Callaghan – a newcomer to the series – is charming as the naive Bertrum Muffet who finds love accidentally with model Sally Martin, played by Jacki Piper, who looks a little uncomfortable here after a good debut in *Up The Jungle*. One of Rothwell's favourite devices – particularly in the 1970s – was the dowdy cygnet that becomes a swan, and here that role is nicely played by Imogen Hassall in her only Carry On film.

Sadly Imogen, who certainly had some talent, was never to break free of her sex kitten image, and committed suicide in 1980. Her scene in the middle of the film, where her attempts to make love to Terry Scott are constantly frustrated by other goings on in the flat she shares with Sally, is excellent, and she holds her own very well with a seasoned performer like Scott. In contrast to the naive Bertrum, Scott's character is using the Bliss agency for nefarious purposes, to have sex with as many women as he can.

Patsy Rowlands is also very funny, giving extra depth to her character as she has done so many times in the series.

Of the regulars, Sid James and Hattie Jacques are both on excellent form, while Charles Hawtrey – in a small, ineffectual role as a private investigator – has little to do, and Joan Sims as Esme exists largely to push the plot along, but as always gives a good performance in this relatively straight role. Bernard Bresslaw, once again, shows what a great character actor he was with another great turn, this time as wrestler Gripper, and overall, this is a decent enough outing in a period of gradual decline.

Carry On Henry (1971)

Distributed by Rank
Produced by Peter Rogers
Directed by Gerald Thomas
Screenplay by Talbot Rothwell
Director of Photography: Alan Hume
Music composed and conducted by Eric Rogers
Filming dates: 12 October 1970 – 27 November 1970
UK release: 3 June 1971, US release: March 1972
Running time: 89 minutes
Budget: £223,000

Cast:
Regulars: Sidney James, Joan Sims, Kenneth Williams, Charles Hawtrey, Terry Scott, Peter Butterworth, Barbara Windsor, Kenneth Connor
Regular supporting cast: Julian Holloway, Patsy Rowlands, Bill Maynard, Derek Francis, Peter Gilmore, Julian Orchard, Margaret Nolan, Billy Cornelius, Alan Curtis, Gertan Klauber
Guests: William Mervyn, Norman Chappell, David Prowse, John Bluthal

Background

As the two-movies per year schedule continued into 1970 and 1971, the team returned to historical subject matter for their much-publicised 21st film. *Henry* followed the success of *Anne Of A Thousand Days* starring Richard Burton in 1969, which had also been shot at Pinewood. Rogers, always one to keep his ear to the ground, once again saw the opportunity to exploit another film's sets and costumes as he had done with *Cleo*. *Carry On Henry* was born, and the cast were even given permission to film in Windsor Great Park and on the Long Walk.

The film itself is an odd curiosity, and it is interesting to imagine what it might have been like had it been shot, say, five years earlier during the golden era of the series. However, with the tone of the series shifting towards overt sex references, the subject of the real Henry's divorce from Catherine of Aragon and marriage to Anne Boleyn was the perfect material to build a sex – or rather lack of sex – comedy around.

The Plot

- Having executed his most recent (unnamed) Queen (Patsy Rowlands), Henry VIII (Sid James) immediately marries the next, Queen Marie of Normandy (Joan Sims). However, Marie loves garlic, eats it before bed and demands that it be put in the food at court.
- The marriage unconsummated, Henry tries everything to get rid of her, even feigning a kidnapping at the hands of Lord Hampton of Wick (Kenneth Connor), who actually plans a plot against the King in reality.

- When Henry is introduced to his next love Bettina (Barbara Windsor) he is resolved to divorce Marie and asks Cromwell (Kenneth Williams) and Wolsey (Terry Scott) to assist. Meanwhile, Sir Roger de Lodgerley (Charles Hawtrey) has impregnated the Queen.
- As political issues close in on him, Henry changes his mind constantly about whether to divorce Marie or not, requiring Roger to face constant torture, either to admit or retract his admission of fatherhood.
- In the end, backed into a corner, Henry resolves to stay with Marie and hands Bettina over to the King of France (Peter Gilmore) once again without consummating his marriage. At the last moment, Henry spots and falls for Catherine Howard and the cycle begins again, but without Cromwell and Wolsey who prefer execution to the prospect of assisting the king further.

Analysis

After the ensemble nature of the last few films, the 21st outing revolves largely around Henry VIII – beautifully played, as ever, by Sid James sporting a rather natty beard – trying to have sex with someone. Anyone. Considering that he is the King, this is an inspired idea. In fact, this might just be his most dominant part in a Carry On, as the plot revolves entirely around his attempts – constantly thwarted – to consummate his marriages to both Marie and Bettina, placing him in almost every scene. He is even thwarted in his attempts to seduce a farmer's daughter, played with gusto by Margaret Nolan. Joan Sims has good fun sporting a comedy French accent as Marie, but the rest of the relatively large cast is slim pickings. In particular, Kenneth Connor, once again, seems to be in the cast only to make up the numbers. Of the supporting players, Peter Gilmore has his best role since *Don't Lose Your Head* as the King of France.

Kenneth Williams and Terry Scott are both ideally cast, with Scott, in particular, having good fun as the duplicitous Wolsey, though both parts are little more than supporting roles.

Henry was the first Carry On to feature extensive nudity, in the sequence where Henry desperately tries to see Bettina naked. Clearly, some of these views are Babs, some of them are a body double, yet they do feel gratuitous, even if they are very discreet to win that all-important 'A' certificate. Appearing halfway through the film, Barbara Windsor nonetheless does an excellent job with very little material, playing knowing innocence with customary skill.

Despite some delightful sets and costumes, and a sumptuous ball scene midway through the film, nothing much happens really. There are no real set pieces, as the plot is all about Henry's political difficulties and his sexual frustration, and the ending is low-key, if nicely ironic. While it all moves along pleasingly enough, this is a Carry On best remembered for its sets and its costumes rather than its comic set pieces or its brilliant dialogue. That said, the script is still funny enough, and Sid's performance is so good that you feel his frustration alongside him. Overall, this is a decent outing, but it might have been better if made during the mid 1960s.

Carry On At Your Convenience (1971)

Distributed by Rank
Produced by Peter Rogers
Directed by Gerald Thomas
Screenplay by Talbot Rothwell
Director of Photography: Ernest Stewart
Music composed and conducted by Eric Rogers
Filming dates: 23 March 1971 – 7 May 1971
UK release: 10 December 1971, US release: not known
Running time: 90 minutes
Budget: £220,000

Cast:
Regulars: Sidney James, Kenneth Williams, Joan Sims, Charles Hawtrey, Hattie Jacques, Bernard Bresslaw
Regular supporting cast: Jacki Piper, Richard O'Callaghan, Patsy Rowlands, Bill Maynard, Renee Houston, Marianne Stone, Margaret Nolan, Julian Holloway, Amelia Bayntun, Hugh Futcher
Guests: Davy Kaye, Kenneth Cope, Anouska Hempel, Philip Stone, Geoffrey Hughes

Background

There had been much publicity surrounding *Carry On Henry*, particularly as it was the 21st Carry On film, although the series 'coming of age' was originally planned to be a work-based comedy. *At Your Convenience* was originally to be called *Carry On Comrade* and much later *Carry On Working*, yet in the end the team settled on the more Anglo-centric title, the use of actual products from a bathroom fittings factory proving a marketing opportunity too good to miss.

The film remains shrouded in controversy, however. Its lack of box office success is usually blamed on its right-wing slant, pouring scorn on trade unions and therefore on the British working class, causing the series 'core demographic' to stay away in droves. Although I believe that the series appeals to a much wider demographic than the working class, there is no doubt that the adverse publicity the film gained for its anti-union stance did it no favours, even though Rothwell had been dropping little 'digs' at the left into his scripts for years.

Readers may remember this throwaway exchange towards the end of *Henry*:

> Lord Hampton of Wick (Kenneth Connor): Your majesty, the Queen has gone into labour!
> King Henry (Sid James): Don't worry, they'll never get back in.

The Plot

- Boggs bathrooms fittings factory.The film follows the fortunes of the factory.
- Following a change in the way tea is served to the workers, shop steward Vic

Spanner (Kenneth Cope) calls the workforce out on strike, aggravated by the arrogance of owner's son Lewis Boggs (Richard O'Callaghan). Lewis is trying to modernise the company by making French-style bidets, against the wishes of his father (Kenneth Williams) and foreman Sid Plummer (Sid James) although designer Charles Coote (Charles Hawtrey) is more enthusiastic.

- Lewis is not taken seriously by the workforce, but has a developing relationship with Sid's daughter, Myrtle (Jacki Piper), who is also pursued by Vic. Sid is married to Beattie (Hattie Jacques) but fancies employee Chloe (Joan Sims), who is married to company sales representative Fred (Bill Maynard).
- Vic is jealous of Lewis dating Myrtle, and follows her, but Lewis pushes his advances too far, and Myrtle rejects him.
- Sid and Beattie's budgie,it seems, can predict winners at the races. Fred wins a bidet contract but needs money quickly to keep the company afloat, so Sid wins it with the help of the budgie.
- Boggs senior plans to sell the company despite protestations of love from his secretary, Miss Withering (Patsy Rowlands).
- Despite the strike, the entire company – management and workers alike – goes on a works outing to Brighton. Myrtle makes Lewis jealous by pretending to like Vic. Lunch cannot be served at their hotel as the catering staff are on strike, to Vic's disgust. Lewis proposes to Myrtle, and beats up Vic. They get married.
- The next morning, Boggs wakes up in Miss Wittering's bed, still determined to sell.
- The wives and girlfriends of the strikers, plus the female staff of the factory, break the strike, and the men follow, humiliating Vic, until he meets the pretty young canteen girl (Anouska Hempel), causing even him to return to work.
- Sid's relationship with Chloe stumbles, but he is made a director as a reward for his financial help and Lewis and Myrtle announce their marriage.
- Vic is a reformed character, and does not strike when given the opportunity.

Analysis

At Your Convenience continues the tone set up by *Loving*, that of a television situation comedy, and within that context, it does fairly well. However, extended over a 90-minute film, this is fairly thin stuff. There are scenarios here that we have seen before: a trip to see a dirty film at the cinema to 'warm up' a girl. (*Camping*); Sid James fancying Joan Sims while married to Hattie Jacques (*Loving*); Patsy Rowlands in love with Kenneth Williams (*Loving*).

This is very much an ensemble film, and although most of the regulars are present, it is the newer cast members that win most of acting honours. Richard O'Callaghan and Jacki Piper continue the chemistry that saw them charm in *Loving*, although O'Callaghan plays a rather less pleasant character here. Patsy Rowlands is given another showcase scene with Kenneth Williams, and it is wonderful, while Renee Houston, making her first appearance in a Carry On since *Spying*, is excellent as Vic's Mother – and Charles Hawtrey's love interest. A great deal of extra footage was shot for this film, unusual for Gerald Thomas, and while some performances usually land on the cutting room floor in a Carry On, here it was Terry Scott's brief appearance as a union bigwig, Mr Allcock, that had to go. Scott was paid £500 for one day's work.

Charles Hawtrey and Kenneth Williams are given little to do in relatively straight supporting roles, and Bernard Bresslaw is similarly underused as Vic's gormless sidekick Bernie.

The villain of the piece – if there is one – is Vic played by Kenneth Cope, in the first of two Carry On appearances. Cope is excellent and Vic is pompous, workshy and hypocritical, but hardly deserving of the beating he is given by Lewis in Brighton, even if he looks none the worse for it a few moments later. Nor does he deserve the spanking he is given by his mother (Renee Houston) late in the film.

His 'conversion' at the end of the film is ridiculous, and although his reason for striking in the first place is also silly, the implication that all industrial disputes can be solved by the common sense of a few determined women is an insult to the audience's intelligence. This is all a serious misstep from Rothwell and something of an insult to the audience, particularly female viewers, facing – as they still do – discrimination in the workplace. What the real-life protagonists of *Made In Dagenham* (2010) who fought for equality in 1968 – just three years before this film was made – would have thought, is not pleasant to contemplate.

That said, the showcase trip to Brighton (and the return journey) is good fun, even if it fails to enhance the story much, apart from getting Lewis and Myrtle married. The storyline between Sid and Chloe (Sid James and Joan Sims, both as good as ever) is well performed and has an unusually sad subtext, since it is clear they both love each other, but the film's moral sensibilities require them to remain with their existing spouses.

Considering that lust is usually king in the 1970s Carry Ons, this is a nice, tender touch. In the end, *At Your Convenience* is a decent enough effort that falls a little flat, not just because of its questionable politics, but because, in Vic Spanner, it sets us up to dislike a character we actually become rather fond of, unbalancing the film. With the benefit of distance, we can see that *At Your Convenience* is flawed but far from terrible.

Carry On Matron (1972)

Distributed by Rank
Produced by Peter Rogers
Directed by Gerald Thomas
Screenplay by Talbot Rothwell
Director of Photography: Ernest Stewart
Music composed and conducted by Eric Rogers
Filming dates: 11 October- 26 November 1971
UK release: 19 May 1972, US release: not known
Running time: 87 minutes
Budget: £224,995

Cast:
Regulars: Sidney James, Kenneth Williams, Joan Sims, Charles Hawtrey, Hattie Jacques, Bernard Bresslaw, Kenneth Connor, Barbara Windsor, Terry Scott
Regular supporting cast: Jacki Piper, Patsy Rowlands, Bill Maynard, Valerie Leon, Michael Nightingale, Derek Francis, Gwendolyn Watts, Margaret Nolan, Jack Douglas, Amelia Bayntun
Guests: Kenneth Cope, Wendy Richard, Madeline Smith

Background

A return to hospital life had been planned since *Again Doctor* in 1969 so it was just a question of when to place it in the schedule. It must have been a relief to return to the wards with *At Your Convenience* having failed at the box office so badly.

Unusually, Talbot Rothwell was not the first choice to pen this film, with Norman Hudis, who had written *Nurse*, of course, the initial writer. However, as a working US resident, the American Screenwriters Guild prevented his participation, and script duties were passed to Rothwell by default. One wonders what sort of fist Hudis might have made of it. Would he have written the film in Rothwell's style, as audiences might have expected, or produced a comedy in keeping with *Nurse*?

As it turned out, Rothwell's take on the subject was as broad as ever, firing off volley after volley of pregnancy jokes, almost like a stand up routine or a sketch show. With the hospital interiors taking on a slightly more contemporary feel, the exteriors were upgraded too, moving from Maidenhead Town Hall – the stand in hospital in *Doctor* and *Again Doctor* – to Heatherwood Hospital in Ascot.

The Plot

- A gang of four robbers (Sid James, Kenneth Cope, Bernard Bresslaw and Bill Maynard) plan to steal contraceptive pills from Finisham Hospital to sell abroad. Although reluctant to be involved, Cyril (Cope) is sent in dressed as a nurse to find where the pills are kept.

- Meanwhile, train conductor Mr. Tidey (Kenneth Connor) waits for his wife (Joan Sims) to give birth. She is 3 weeks overdue and eats constantly.
- Head consultant at the hospital, Sir Bernard Cutting is a hypochondriac, convinced that he needs to prove himself sexually as he may be becoming feminine.
- Psychiatrist Dr. Goode (Charles Hawtrey) shares a secret with Matron (Hattie Jacques) – they watch a medical soap opera together.
- Cyril, in drag, fights off the attentions of Dr Prodd (Terry Scott) and falls for Nurse Ball (Barbara Windsor) with whom he shares a room. After getting in the newspapers for having delivered the triplets of celebrity Jane Darling (Valerie Leon), Cyril accidentally reveals that he is a man to Nurse Ball.
- Seeing Cyril's father in the hospital, Matron smells a rat and pursues him.
- Cutting decides that he loves Matron, and in a jealous rage confronts Goode, only stopping when he realises that they are both freemasons ('Newts').
- Just as Cutting proposes to Matron, the gang enter the hospital in disguise, blowing open the pill store, and the explosion brings on Mrs. Tidey's baby.
- A chase ensues, and the gang are caught but allowed to escape as Cutting and Matron fear the shame that the revelation of Cyril's masculinity would bring to the hospital.
- Matron and Cutting marry.

Analysis

Once again the lead role of Cyril is given to Kenneth Cope . His character is rather more likeable this time out, one of the series' more convincing transvestites, given that he spends most of the film in drag. Hattie Jacques makes her fourth appearance as a Matron – five if you include *Camping* – in an enhanced role and, amusingly, gets her man this time out, having loved a variation on the same Kenneth Williams character so many times in the past.

Of the rest of the ensemble, most of the regulars get very little screen time, with Hawtrey and Bresslaw particularly underused, although Connor is good in a supporting role as the long-suffering Mr Tidey. Kenneth Williams shows the signs of overplaying, as he regularly did in the 1970s, slipping out of character to bring us 'Snide' perhaps a little too often, although Sid James has great fun in the final chase sequence playing a bearded Austrian Doctor. Once again, Terry Scott plays a less-than-pleasant character, the predatory Dr Prodd. Jacki Piper makes her last Carry On appearance, in a fairly straight role as Sister and one of the great supporting players in Carry On films Michael Nightingale – usually only glimpsed as a glorified extra since his first appearance in *Regardless* – has an entire scene with Kenneth Williams, and very good he is too.

Despite all the 'unwanted pregnancy' jokes, the film is actually quite sweet, and while there are plenty of young women to be seen – Valerie Leon makes another appearance and starlet Madeline Smith makes her only appearance in the series – the fact that they are all clutching babies desexualises them somewhat, which is quite refreshing in a Carry On.

Jack Douglas makes his first appearance in the series as his twitching 'Alf' character, a sort of 'live' audition for later films. His one-minute cameo – with Kenneth Connor reacting to his twitching with some of his own – is genuinely funny, and it is no wonder that he was to become a regular for the rest of the series.

Carry On Matron is a perfectly decent, if minor, addition to the series. While it is hard to find too many faults with the film, nor does it have any stand-out performances, sequences or lines, and of the four hospital-set films, it is the least consequential. Perhaps this is because there are so many tropes we have seen before in the series, from a hypochondriac (*Sergeant*) to a scene where a woman is disturbed in her bath (*Doctor*) to a man in drag being mistaken for a woman (*Screaming*, *Don't Lose Your Head* and – let's face it – most of the rest of the series). Better was to follow.

Carry On Abroad (1972)

Distributed by Rank
Produced by Peter Rogers
Directed by Gerald Thomas
Screenplay by Talbot Rothwell
Director of Photography: Alan Hume
Music composed and conducted by Eric Rogers
Filming dates: 17 April to 26 May 1972
UK release: 15 December 1972, US release: 8 December 1973
Running time: 88 minutes
Budget: £225,000

Cast:
Regulars: Sidney James, Kenneth Williams, Joan Sims, Charles Hawtrey, Hattie Jacques, Bernard Bresslaw, Kenneth Connor, Barbara Windsor, Peter Butterworth
Regular supporting cast: Patsy Rowlands, Derek Francis, Jack Douglas, Gertan Klauber, Hugh Futcher, Alan Curtis, June Whitfield, Amelia Bayntun
Guests: Jimmy Logan, Sally Geeson, Carol Hawkins, Gail Grainger, John Clive, David Kernan, Ray Brooks

Background

Carry On Abroad was the last film to be made on the six-monthly treadmill that had seen sixteen films made in little more than eight years. It takes as its subject the relatively new trend of overseas package holidays and the bad press some operators received in the early 1970s for poor service and partially built hotels. Members of the cast – like June Whitfield, returning for her first Carry On since *Nurse* thirteen years earlier – hoped that the subject matter might allow for a foreign location. No such luck, and a corner of the car park at Pinewood was filled with sand for the location shoot during a particularly chilly English Spring.

The Plot

- A party of tourists prepare for a short break in the Mediterranean resort of Elsbels.
- It includes: Vic Flange and his wife Cora. Vic is hoping to go away with a potential mistress Sadie (Barbara Windsor) before Cora arranges to come along at the last minute; Mother's boy and secret drunk Eustace Tuttle (Charles Hawtrey); Stanley Blunt (Kenneth Connor) and his stuck-up wife Evelyn (June Whitfield); Bachelor on the make Bert (Jimmy Logan); a gay couple Robin and Nicholas (John Clive and David Kernan); two young women Lily and Marge (Sally Geeson and Carol Hawkins); a group of monks including Brother Bernard (Bernard Bresslaw) who is uncertain about his faith. The party is led by Stuart (Kenneth Williams) and his assistant Moira Plunkett (Gail Grainger).

- The hotel is unfinished, and their hosts – Pepe and Floella (Peter Butterworth and Hattie Jacques) – are barely ready for them. Despite numerous complaints, the holidaymakers settle in.
- Sid neglects Cora in pursuit of Sadie, who is more interested in Bert. Stanley shows interest in Cora. Bernard falls for Marge despite warnings from the leader of his group (Derek Francis).
- Nicholas shows interest in Lily, angering Robin. It rains, so an excursion to the local village is organised, ending with the entire party spending the night in jail.
- Moira disappears with the Chief of Police (Alan Curtis), 'persuading' him to be lenient. Evelyn stays behind, and is seduced by Georgio, a member of the hotel staff (Ray Brooks).
- Stanley returns to find her a changed woman. The rain continues, and with a farewell party going badly, various holidaymakers spike the punch, livening things up considerably.
- Bernard decides to leave the order to go out with Marge. The rain begins to destroy the hotel, seeping into the foundations, despite Pepe's efforts to stop the destruction.
- The holidaymakers pair off as the hotel collapses. Vic stays with Cora, while Bert and Sadie get together and Stuart and Moira also pair off, still ignoring Pepe as the hotel collapses. A little while later, the entire group reassembled at Vic's pub, where Stuart now works, declaring the holiday a great success.

Analysis

Terry Scott had departed the series following his appearance in *Matron*. He was a big television star by the early 1970s, but even without him *Abroad* was the only film in the entire series to feature all nine of the 'dream team' of James, Williams, Sims, Hawtrey, Jacques, Bresslaw, Connor, Windsor and Butterworth. In particular, the film sees a welcome return to Peter Butterworth, his first decent part in a Carry On since *Camping* in 1969. The supporting cast rings the changes, too. As well as June Whitfield, the team cast Scottish comedian Jimmy Logan in a meaty role as Sid James' love rival. Also involved are the series' first openly gay couple, played by the talented John Clive – a regular on British television throughout the 1970s – and singer/actor David Kernan, albeit with a somewhat dubious bisexual subtext. Glamour is provided by two more well-known television starlets, Carol Hawkins and Sally Geeson. Sally was already known for playing Sid James' daughter in *Bless This House*, also to be filmed by Rogers within a few months, and had appeared as a schoolgirl in *Regardless* ten years earlier, while Carol Hawkins was already a well-known name in British comedy. Actress Gail Grainger makes her only appearance in the series as the liberated Miss Plunkett. *Abroad* is also the only film in the series to feature Ray Brooks, who became another well-known name in British television, mainly for his vocal work. The year before, he had narrated the children's cartoon series *Mr Benn*, the role for which he remains best known, despite a lengthy career in film and television.

Abroad is the last great Carry On film, and looking at it within the context of the few films that came before it, it is difficult to know precisely where such a level of inspiration came from.

Furthermore, the film is by no means the funniest, has few quotable lines, has location work that is unconvincing, and yet it really satisfies. Part of this is down to the huge influx of new blood, of course, who rise to the occasion expertly marshalled by the always-fatherly Gerald Thomas.

But the film would not work without the right balance between the principals, and whereas in the past some of the bigger stars might have been underused – particularly Bernard Bresslaw, partially due to Rothwell's tendency in later years to give so much screen time to Sid James – each of them gets some moment to shine.

A great deal of credit must go to Peter Butterworth and Hattie Jacques as the owners of Paradise Hotel in Elsbels. This is a Hattie that we have never seen before, a fiery Mediterranean brunette. Hers is a great performance with huge amounts of energy. Butterworth, too, sustains a version of English of which Stanley Unwin might have been proud. Rothwell's script may be lacking great lines, but it provides the right structure for the various plot threads to come together. Bresslaw's storyline, as the uncertain monk who discovers love with Carol Hawkins, is very sweet.

Many of the other stars deliver performances that are comforting in their familiarity. Sid has his usual problems: stuck with Joan Sims while fancying Barbara Windsor, who, in turn, pursues Jimmy Logan. Charles Hawtrey is constantly drunk (like his character in *Cowboy*), with an odd passion for leapfrog, while Kenneth Connor – in his best role since *Cleo* – plays repressed passion to perfection 'I've forgotten what you do!'

Barbara Windsor also has her best part in a Carry On to date, a more worldly character befitting a woman in her mid-30s.

The final sequence – when the holidaymakers are too drunk to assist poor Pepe as the hotel disintegrates – is very similar to the climax of *Up the Khyber*, although it is drunkenness rather that the British stiff upper lip which causes him to be ignored on this occasion. Indeed, the reason that *Abroad* works so well is because it feels like a Carry On greatest hits package – even Eric Rogers throws in some of his old themes into his exuberant score. As a film it is far from a perfect, but as summation of all that is good about the Talbot Rothwell-scripted era, it works just fine.

Carry On Girls (1973)

Distributed by Rank
Produced by Peter Rogers
Directed by Gerald Thomas
Screenplay by Talbot Rothwell
Director of Photography: Alan Hume
Music composed and conducted by Eric Rogers
Filming dates: 16 April to 25 May 1973
UK release: 9 November 1973, US release: not known
Running time: 88 minutes
Budget: £205,962

Cast:
Regulars: Sidney James, Joan Sims, Bernard Bresslaw, Kenneth Connor, Barbara Windsor, Peter Butterworth
Regular supporting cast: Patsy Rowlands, Jack Douglas, Joan Hickson, David Lodge, Valerie Leon, Margaret Nolan, Marianne Stone, Michael Nightingale, Patricia Franklin, Billy Cornelius, Hugh Futcher
Guests: Jimmy Logan, June Whitfield, Sally Geeson, Wendy Richard, Arnold Ridley, Robin Asquith, Bill Pertwee, Brenda Cowling, Angela Grant, Pauline Peart

The Plot

- Fircombe, a fading seaside town with a terrible sunshine record.
- To bring new visitors to the Town, local businessman and councillor Sidney Fiddler (Sid James) plans a beauty contest, despite the objections of feminist Augusta Prodworthy (June Whitfield).
- He asks Peter Potter (Bernard Bresslaw) to do the P.R. despite the anger of Peter's fiancée the dowdy Paula Perkins (Valerie Leon).
- They use the hotel of Connie Philpotts (Joan Sims) as a base, despite her protestations. At a photo shoot at the hotel two of the contestants, Hope Springs (Barbara Windsor) and Dawn Brakes (Margaret Nolan), fight, gaining publicity for the event.
- Meanwhile the feminist group plan to further humiliate the Mayor (Kenneth Connor), having disrupted the opening of a men's toilet, by also disrupting an opening at the local maternity hospital.
- They succeed. A television studio shows interest, and a publicity event is arranged. Sid, Peter and Hope devise a plan for a man to infiltrate the event to be unmasked to help with publicity. Peter is selected as the 'girl' and is unmasked as planned, and a chase ensues, but Peter escapes.
- The planned publicity is achieved, with the mystery of Peter / Patricia still unsolved. Paula arrives unexpectedly, and agrees to swap places with Peter after Hope fills her in. She is – of course – gorgeous.
- Mildred (Patsy Rowlands), the Mayor's wife, joins the feminist group.
- Paula and Peter are reconciled.

- The day of the contest arrives, and the feminist group create havoc, beginning with sprinkling itching powder and finally flooding the theatre.
- The boorish crowd demand their money back and round on Sid, who escapes with Hope on her motorbike, even though Connie has stolen the door money.

Analysis

The extended period between filming *Abroad* and *Girls* – almost exactly one year – meant that there were further changes in the air in the Carry On camp. Charles Hawtrey had been dropped from the series due to his excessive drinking, although Hawtrey maintained – in a later interview – that he wanted to leave due to the increasing lack of subtlety in Rothwell's scripts, the double entendres having been replaced by single ones. However, Kenneth Williams was also unavailable, committed to a stage part, despite attempts to entice him. These changes left some holes in the production. Arguably, though, this was for the better.

While *Abroad* had coped well with a huge ensemble cast, other recent films had not been so successful. The smaller cast of regulars in *Girls* allowed some talented performers who had not had much screen time of late – specifically Kenneth Connor and Bernard Bresslaw – to thrive on bigger and better roles. Connor is excellent – as he always is – in a very amusing part, as Frederick Bumble, the pompous Mayor of Fircombe who takes his duties very seriously. His tiny moustache is a perfect touch. In fact, as a satire of small-town politics, it is surprisingly accurate, and no wonder, since Rothwell had been a town clerk in Brighton during the 1930s. What a shame there was never a 'Carry On Up the Council'.

Bresslaw, too, gets a lot more screen time than usual – required, once again, to dress up as a deeply implausible woman. Played by another actor, his character would have been hard to like, but Bernie could make a vicious killer accessible (and did a couple of times) and here you cannot help but like P.R. man Peter Potter.

I like *Carry On Girls* despite its controversial subject matter, a small-time beauty pageant in a dreary seaside town, which conveniently allows huge amounts of barely-covered, wobbling female flesh to be on display for most of its duration. In terms of the joke content, there are many chuckles, if few belly laughs, and the film moves along at such a zip that if the viewer doesn't like one 'bristols' joke, another one will be along pretty quickly, and there are a lot of jokes about breasts in this film. There is that notorious cat fight, and so many slapped bottoms that Sid James would be arrested for sexual harassment in the 21st century.

But actually, there is rather more going on here than meets the eye. As well as the bevvy of women on display, there is also the first feminist group in Carry On, and indeed the first lesbian, in Patricia Franklin's Rosemary, although direct references to her sexuality are avoided. Rothwell allows the feminists to 'win' in the end – as usual, the women are seen as cleverer than the men – but he still cannot help sending them up. In the scene where the excellent Patsy Rowlands burns her bra, the resulting fire produces panic and a call to the fire brigade, at that very moment, being inspected by her husband, the Mayor.

Rowlands' role is an interesting one, here. Her character is not just downtrodden by her pompous husband; she may even be clinically depressed, until the feminist group gives her life new meaning and the opportunity for revenge. Hers is an unusually nuanced performance for a Carry On.

There are also a few other performances worth noting. Dad's Army veteran Arnold Ridley has a one-line cameo as an elderly councillor. Peter Butterworth steals every scene he is in as a randy old man living in Joan Sims' hotel. Joan Hickson is superb as a dotty old lady in a part originally planned for Renee Houston, while David Lodge also fills in as a police inspector in a part originally planned for Bill Maynard before a television role got in the way. Jack Douglas is funny in a bigger role than his two previous appearances in *Matron* and *Abroad*, as is a well-cast Robin Asquith. June Whitfield is wonderful as the ironically named Augusta Prodworthy and also dubs Valerie Leon's part. It is unclear why this was necessary. Perhaps Valerie's performance wasn't quite right, or perhaps her voice was a touch too sexy for the pre-transformation version of Paula.

The film also includes the first black female character to not play a cannibal, albeit a nonspeaking one, in Pauline Peart. Quite an achievement for this most conservative of series.

Then there is the ongoing, multi-film love triangle between Sid James, Joan Sims and Barbara Windsor. Sid starts off with Joan, but in the end ends up with Babs – at last. In the context of the film, this works since here Barbara shifts her screen persona from the innocence of the late 1960s to the more worldly character hinted at in *Matron* and expanded upon in *Abroad*.

For Joan Sims, this is a difficult film, giving her little to work with, except to grow steadily angrier as Sid and the girls gradually trash her hotel and drive out her regular guests. There is, however, a sting in the tale, as Sid rushes to the pier box office to take the receipts of the aborted show, only to find that Joan has got to them before him.

In a scene reminiscent of *Cowboy*, he and Babs disappear into the sunset on her motorbike leaving others to deal with the chaos.

Despite the familiarity of many of the set pieces and the gratuitous display of titillating female flesh, *Carry On Girls* is an entertaining, surprisingly witty and well-structured film that deserves a better reputation.

Carry On Dick (1974)

Distributed by Rank
Produced by Peter Rogers
Directed by Gerald Thomas
Screenplay by Talbot Rothwell, from a treatment by George Evans and Lawrie Wyman
Director of Photography: Ernest Steward
Music composed and conducted by Eric Rogers
Filming dates: 4 March – 11 April 1974
UK release: 12 July 1974, US release: 25 December 1974
Running time: 91 minutes
Budget: £245,000

Cast:
Regulars: Sidney James, Joan Sims, Bernard Bresslaw, Barbara Windsor, Peter Butterworth, Kenneth Connor, Hattie Jacques
Regular supporting cast: Jack Douglas, David Lodge, Margaret Nolan, Marianne Stone, Michael Nightingale, Patsy Rowlands, Bill Maynard, Bill Cornelius
Guests: John Clive, Sam Kelly, George Moon, Eva Reuben-Staier, Brian Coburn

The Plot

- Dick Turpin (Sid James) – also the local rector – is a highwayman causing havoc by stealing from the rich, assisted by Tom (Peter Butterworth) and Harriett (Barbara Windsor). When Sir Roger Daley, the head of the Bow Street Runners (Bernard Bresslaw), suffers from Dick's activities at first hand, he dispatches his lieutenants, Captain Fancy (Kenneth Williams) and Sergeant Jock Strapp (Jack Douglas), to catch him.
- They first attempt to snare him at the Old Cock Inn, based on information that 'Big Dick' has a birthmark in an 'unusual' place.
- Turpin contrives to throw then off the scent, humiliating them at every turn, even having them falsely arrested by the local constable (Kenneth Connor).
- By a stroke of luck for the Runners, Harriett is arrested and Dick and Tom are forced to rescue her, posing as women. Pursued to the local rectory, they once again escape and head to Scotland and safety. Dick and Harriett consummate their relationship.

Analysis

Several factors conspired to make *Carry On Dick* the end of an era. Peter Rogers had asked the writers of the popular radio series *The Navy Lark*, George Evans and Lawrie Wyman, to come up with some Carry On ideas after they had submitted a script based on *The Navy Lark* theme. They came up with a treatment – and indeed a full script – for a film based on the Dick Turpin legend. Rogers and Thomas liked the idea but passed on the script, handing it to Rothwell instead.

Unfortunately, years of writing solo to strict deadlines had begun to take their toll on the scribe, and he failed to finish the script, succumbing to nervous exhaustion, and aside from a couple of scripts for Frankie Howerd, he never wrote anything substantial again, although he was awarded an O.B.E. in 1977.

Ironically, he was about to sign a new, long term contract with Rogers to write the next few Carry On films. The script for *Dick* was compiled by his daughter from his notes and dictation based on the work he had already completed, then handed to Rogers to finalise.

Carry On Dick was also to be the last proper Carry On to feature Sid James and Barbara Windsor, although Babs was to co-present *That's Carry On* in 1978. Sid was unavailable for *Behind* due to a theatre tour in Australia, and died in 1976 just as it was in pre-production.

The filming of *Dick* coincided with the London run of the stage show *Carry On London*, which featured Sid, Babs, Kenneth Connor, Bernard Bresslaw, Peter Butterworth, and Jack Douglas on stage eight times per week for an eighteen-month run. *Dick* featured all six of these actors, requiring filming to be over in time for them to get back to the Victoria Palace Theatre for the first show. While the performances of most of the actors seems unaffected by the schedule, the same cannot be said – sadly – for Sid James, who gives a lethargic performance bereft of his usual energy. The only scenes where he seems at his best, are (not surprisingly) the one to one encounters with Barbara Windsor. Elsewhere he seems tired, his voice croaky.

In fact, *Dick* is not the greatest of outings, even though the cast do their very best with thin material. Jack Douglas is very good in his largest Carry On part, wisely keeping the twitches to a minimum, and Kenneth Connor gives another expert characterisation. Peter Butterworth is underused, as is Joan Sims, who was often so after *Up The Khyber*. Hattie Jacques plays her usual role – a reliable servant with hidden passions. However, Rothwell's plot structure is not dissimilar to *Don't Lose Your Head*, with Kenneth Williams in the same role, and Bernard Bresslaw able to get his teeth into a rare authority figure as his boss. In the best Carry Ons the jokes come thick and fast, and in *Dick*, while there are a few decent exchanges here and there, any humour there is comes from situations rather than one-liners.

There's a running joke about Sir Roger Daley (Bresslaw) being held up and left naked, which amuses, and part of the climax, which involves the air pump on the church organ repeatedly dying, is also funny, but there is only so far you can take variations on jokes around the word 'dick' and make them amusing. Despite the undeniable chemistry between them, the relationship between Sid and Babs is slightly disturbing compared to Girls, with Barbara playing a fully-fledged youthful nymphomaniac pursuing the 61-year-old Sid.

It is a shame that Sid's last Carry On should neither be the finest film nor his best performance. Had his last film been *Girls*, we would, at least, have seen a Sid James performance in the classic style, with him and Babs riding into the sunset. Of course, they do that at the end, *Dick* too, but here it doesn't feel quite ... right.

Carry On Behind (1975)

Distributed by Rank
Produced by Peter Rogers
Directed by Gerald Thomas
Screenplay by Dave Freeman
Director of Photography: Ernest Steward
Music composed and conducted by Eric Rogers
Filming dates: March 1975 – April 1975
UK release: 19 December 1975, 2 April 1976
Running time: 90 minutes
Budget: £217,000

Cast:
Regulars: Kenneth Williams, Joan Sims, Bernard Bresslaw, Peter Butterworth, Kenneth Connor
Regular supporting cast: Jack Douglas, David Lodge, Marianne Stone, Patsy Rowlands, Liz Fraser, Patricia Franklin, Brian Osborne, Larry Dann, Larry Martyn, Billy Cornelius, Alexandra Dane, Hugh Futcher
Guests: Elke Sommer, Windsor Davies, Sam Kelly, Carol Hawkins, Sherrie Hewson, Ian Lavender, Adrienne Posta, Sam Kelly, Johnny Briggs, Brenda Cowling, Donald Hewlett, Georgina Moon

The Plot

- Professor Crump (Kenneth Williams) travels to a caravan site with open-minded new colleague Anna Vooshka (Elke Sommer) in search of Roman artefacts. With his own caravan damaged, he and Anna have to share one rented from the camp odd job man Henry (Peter Butterworth).
- Also travelling to the site are Fred and Ernie (Windsor Davies and Jack Douglas), two married men on the make, and pursuing Sandra and Carol (Carol Hawkins and Sherrie Hewson). Also at the site are Arthur and Linda Upmore (Bernard Bresslaw and Patsy Rowlands), there with their bad-tempered mother Daphne (Joan Sims) and her Minah bird and Joe and Norma Baxter (Ian Lavender and Adrienne Posta), who have a large dog. The camp is run by Major Leep (Kenneth Connor).
- A gas explosion caused by Daphne causes Sandra and Carol to lose their tent and also causes Crump to believe he has had an accident, found to be untrue when examined by a local doctor (George Layton).
- He also accidentally sets off a water main while digging within the campsite. Both the Minah bird and the dog cause misunderstandings and chaos, as does a missing sign to the men's showers.
- Major Leep attempts to seduce Daphne but is rejected. Henry, it turns out, is Daphne's estranged husband. They rekindle their relationship.
- At a dance at the site, freshly painted chairs cause everyone to stick to them. Leep realises that he has accidentally booked a stripper as the entertainment.

That night, huge holes appeared all over the site, which was once a Roman mine. Fred and Ernie get a visit from their wives, while Crump and Anna become good friends, piecing together an erotic mosaic.

- Sandra and Carol leave with students working on the dig.

Analysis

With Talbot Rothwell unable to continue with his writing duties, Peter Rogers asked Dave Freeman to adapt a script he had already written called *Love On Wheels* as a Carry On, to be set in a caravan park. Freeman was already a hard-working comedy writer, having initially written for Benny Hill, and he went on to write for a variety of comedy performers as well as for sitcoms, including the Sid James vehicle *Bless This House*. He also had Carry On experience, having written the rather suspect script for *Carry On Again Christmas* in 1970.

Freeman's script for *Carry On Behind* captures the essence of a Rothwell script quite nicely, albeit one of his saucier efforts. What it does not have is the zip of even the worst Rothwell efforts, however, and there really aren't enough decent one-liners. Furthermore, there is a feeling of desperation in the writing – a need to get to the 'funny bit ' without any build-up to it. The opening sequence is quite a nice idea – that Professor Crump gives a lecture without checking that the film his audience is watching is a striptease by mistake, and the way it develops when he does realise is nicely done, but was there any need for him to knock everything over at the start as well?

Similarly, Anna's bizarre way of speaking English is a standard low-comedy device, but here it seems tacked on and becomes tiresome very quickly, despite the charm and commitment in Elke Sommer's performance. The Baxters only exist as characters to allow their dog to run amok, while Bernard Bresslaw – never a bland actor – is stuck with a character with no real personality. Although the Carry On films are not intended to be realistic, there has to be something in the plot and characterisation to be plausible at least, and in *Behind* there is just not enough to make us believe that these are even possibly real people in real situations. Most of the set pieces come about through the actions of either a large dog or a Minah bird with a potty mouth.

There are exceptions. The subplot between Joan Sims and Peter Butterworth as a separated husband and wife reunited after ten years is tenderly handled. It is clearly a relic of Freeman's previous script, as it is tonally completely unlike anything in a Hudis-era script, let alone a Rothwell one. Butterworth has some nice moments in the film, but until the transformation in her character towards the end, once again Joan Sims is poorly treated by the script, asked to play Patsy Rowlands' mother, even though the actresses were only one year apart in age.

Windsor Davies is excellent in a part clearly intended for Sid James, playing nicely against a rather more broadly comic performance from Jack Douglas in the traditional 'Bresslaw sidekick' role. One almost wishes that Bresslaw himself had played that role. Kenneth Connor, as usual, is excellent as the pompous yet lovelorn Major, delivering the best line in the film when spurned by Joan Sims with superb pathos and timing: 'But I don't want it all. I just want a bit!'

Kenneth Williams, however, mugs his way through an implausible role as an academic buffoon, while the rest of the cast is made up from television regulars, including Ian Lavender from *Dad's Army*, married to a preposterously coiffured Adrienne Posta. My favourite moment in the film is a brief one, and once again very British. Spotting Anna in the men's shower:

Joe (Ian Lavender) – with a stage-whisper: Is that a woman?
Arthur (Bernard Bresslaw) – also with a stage-whisper: Yes!
Joe: Bloody hell!

There's nothing particularly funny about this exchange, but there is a truth there that really appeals, and might not have been found in a Rothwell script.

But in the main, this is a lacklustre remake or *Carry On Camping* which was released only six years previously, let us not forget.

Despite the quality of Davies' performance, the film desperately needs Sid James and Barbara Windsor, who were both unavailable due to theatre commitments. The film is watchable and mildly amusing, but any production that feels the need to end the entire film on one of its main actors' catchphrases – in this case, Kenneth Williams' 'No, stop messin' about' – is probably not as good as it needs to be.

Carry On England (1976)

Distributed by Rank
Produced by Peter Rogers
Directed by Gerald Thomas
Screenplay by David Pursall and Jack Seddon
Director of Photography: Ernest Steward
Music composed and conducted by Max Harris
Filming dates: 3 May 1976 – 4 June 1976
UK release: 31 October 1976, US release: 19 November 1976
Running time: 89 minutes
Budget: £250,000

Cast:
Regulars: Joan Sims, Peter Butterworth, Kenneth Connor
Regular supporting cast: Jack Douglas, David Lodge, Patricia Franklin, Brian Osborne, Larry Dann, Julian Holloway, Michael Nightingale, Johnny Briggs
Guests: Windsor Davies, Patrick Mower, Judy Geeson, Peter Jones, Diane Langton, Mervyn Hayes, Tricia Newby

The Plot

- 1940. 1313 Experimental Artillery Battery are a continuing problem so the Brigadier (Peter Jones) dispatches Captain S. Melly (Kenneth Connor), feeling that ignorance is the only option he has, having tried every other tactic.
- Melly arrives to find the unit in a shambolic state. Despite the ineffectual but loud Sergeant-Major 'Tiger' Bloomer (Windsor Davies), lusted after by Private Jennifer Foukkes-Sharp (Joan Sims), the mixed unit have paired off, and spend all their time 'at it', led by Sergeants Willing and Able (Patrick Mower and Judy Geeson) and twitchy Bombardier Ready (Jack Douglas).
- The pompous and over officious Melly attempts to lick the unit into shape, but is sabotaged at every turn,
- Melly suffering a series of humiliating pratfalls and practical jokes. He uses barbed wire to keep the men and women apart, though they both dig tunnels, ending up in each other's huts.
- An anti-aircraft gun arrives, allowing the unit to practice with real equipment, but Melly is again humiliated when the Brigadier arrives for inspection. However, when a real air raid occurs, the group perform well.
- Tiger and Jennifer embrace, together at last.
- Melly, due to a finger injury, invents the V for Victory sign, later stolen by Churchill.

Discussions about the worst film in the 31-movie series usually polarise around the final three: *Columbus*, *Emmannuelle* and this outing *Carry On England*. It is not hard to understand why. With a few exceptions in an otherwise barren script, this is mirth-free stuff from beginning to end.

Originally intended as an edition of *Carry On Laughing,* Peter Rogers suggested that Pursall and Seddon expand the film into a full Carry On script. The film, once made, caused the censor some issues, and it is not hard to see why. Some gratuitous bare breasts and a dubious use of the word 'Fokker' by Patrick Mower threatened an 'AA' certificate in the UK, although both censored and uncensored versions of the film can now be viewed on the DVD version with PG certificates.

The film has numerous other problems. First of all, it is made very clear that we are supposed to root for the members of 1313 squadron against the officious Melly, yet they are a selfish shambles, and the viewer, in fact, has some sympathy with Melly's mission to make them into a useful unit, particularly as the role is played by the much-loved Kenneth Connor, giving the part everything as always. Windsor Davies is actually very good as the Sergeant Major, played as a carbon copy of his character in the television series *It Ain't Half Hot, Mum,* but if he is so authoritarian, why hasn't the unit responded?

Aside from a largely joke-free script, one of the main problems lies in the casting of the supporting players, however. Although they do not give bad performances per se, Judy Geeson and Patrick Mower, neither best known for their comic roles, seem out of place here, neither especially likeable or sympathetic. Joan Sims, a leading player only a few years earlier, is buried in a humiliating supporting role in which her main character trait is her bulk. The rest of the battery is made up of occasional Carry On supporting players, the most notable being Patricia Franklin and Larry Dann, while Peter Butterworth and Julian Holloway are wasted in tiny supporting roles. As a result, the film is left to Connor and Davies to hold the comedy together, and while they both do their best, it is an uphill fight. Dull rather than inept, with a poor script and dubious casting, this is a poor film.

That's Carry On (1977)

Distributed by Rank
Produced by Peter Rogers
Compiled and directed by Gerald Thomas
Screenplay by Tony Church
Director of Photography: Tony Imi
Music composed and conducted by Eric Rogers
Filming dates: 12 July – 13 July 1977
UK release: November 1977, US release: 10 March 1979
Running time: 95 minutes
Budget: £30,000

Cast:
Regulars: Kenneth Williams, Barbara Windsor

Analysis

As always, Peter Rogers knew an opportunity when he saw one, and had noted, with interest, how successful the two big-screen compilations of classic Hollywood clips had been, *That's Entertainment Parts 1* and *2*, from 1974 and 1976 respectively. Having opened up communications with Nat Cohen of EMI, whose Anglo-Amalgamated had released the first twelve films before the death of Stuart Levy, he now saw an opportunity for his own compilation of every film in the series to date. Gerald Thomas set about compiling the footage.

So, Barbara Windsor and Kenneth Williams were shepherded into the projection room at Pinewood to shoot two days of links, or "interruptions" as the film calls them. We know that Kenneth Williams was paid £2000 for his (admittedly fairly gruelling) two days. He and Babs played with Tony Church's rather corny script to make it more user-friendly, but there is still a tone about their dialogue that grates. Aside from Kenneth Williams' consumption of a food hamper and some champagne, the links do have some sort of narrative. About 30 minutes from the end, Kenneth needs to visit the bathroom. Babs doesn't let him go, and when she leaves, he can't get out, and during the closing titles it is clearly implied that he has wet himself, making for a rather strange, off-color ending, even for a Carry On.

The clips themselves concentrate largely on physical humour and pratfalls, particularly where certain films are only given a few moments of screen time, as in *Cruising*. In other cases, as with *Doctor* or *Cleo*, better-known or better-loved films, the clips act as little summaries of the films themselves, including some of the best-known moments. In later films, the supposedly sexier moments – Barbara Windsor in the shower in *Abroad*, for instance – are also given priority.

Structurally, after a worrying opening title sequence that features as many bare bottoms as possible, the film kicks off with sequences from *Don't Lose Your Head*, *Follow that Camel* and *Doctor*, before moving through the early films in chronological sequence, with longer selections per film from *Spying* onwards.

There are a few nuances. *Up The Khyber*, widely considered The team's finest achievement bookends the film. There is a brief clip at the start and a longer sequence at the end, which includes the famous dinner scene, also often considered the Carry On series' finest individual moment. *At Your Convenience* is buried in a very short sequence just before the end, most likely because of its poor box office showing and a feeling that a section should be featured for completion's sake, even if it was considered an embarrassment at the time. *England* is not featured in the film, most probably for practical rather than artistic reasons, as production on both films will probably have overlapped.

Despite the somewhat misjudged linking sections, *That's Carry On* is an impressive achievement, with commercial impact in mind, distilling 28 films into 90 minutes, even if the early films do not get the screen time their quality deserves. It was not a commercial success, and aside from its DVD release, it has been superseded by the *What A Carry On* compilation shows.

Carry On Emmannuelle (1978)

Distributed by Hemdale
Produced by Peter Rogers
Directed by Gerald Thomas
Screenplay by Lance Peters (additional material from Peter Rogers, Vince Powell and Willy Rushton)
Director of Photography: Alan Hume
Music composed and conducted by Eric Rogers.
Song 'Love Crazy' by Kenny Lynch.
Filming dates: 10 April 1978 – 15 May 1978
UK release: 24 November 1978, US release: 7 December 1978
Running time: 88 minutes
Budget: £320,000

Cast:
Regulars: Kenneth Williams, Joan Sims, Peter Butterworth, Kenneth Connor, Jack Douglas
Regular supporting cast: Larry Dann, Eric Barker, Victor Maddern, Michael Nightingale
Guests: Susan Danielle, Beryl Reid, Henry Magee, Robert Dorning, Dino Shafeek, Tricia Newby, Norman Mitchell, Corbett Woodall

Background

It is a shame that the series should end – for 14 years, at least – with a whimper rather than a bang. In fact, one might even ask, 'What were they thinking?' To answer that, some context is needed so that mitigation can be offered. The *Emmanuelle* soft porn films – starring Sylvia Kristel, initially – were already starting to blossom into a profitable series in their own right. Let us not forget that these films did not play on the sex film circuit, but to mainstream audiences, as did (to a lesser extent) the large number of British sex comedies released during the 1970s. These generally featured casual nudity and unlikely sex scenes against a Carry On–style backdrop, and featured many of the popular British actors and actresses who make occasional appearances in the Carry On series. A quick glance at the cast list of *Confessions of a Driving Instructor* reveals Ian Lavender, Liz Fraser, Bill Maynard, Windsor Davies and Irene Handl – all veterans of the Carry Ons. It must have been very tempting, therefore, for Peter Rogers and his team to want to cash in on such an apparent money-spinner.

But how to combine sex with family entertainment? Perhaps naively, they believed it could be done, and Lance Peters was commissioned to write a script. New backers Cleve Investments specifically requested more Carry On regulars, and so alongside the four that had appeared in the disappointing *Carry On England,* both Kenneth Williams and Barbara Windsor were asked to return – Williams only agreeing after an increase in his usual fee was negotiated.

Barbara was unable to appear due to a change in the filming schedule, which is a shame – she would certainly have livened the scenes she was due to appear in; three of the mid-film fantasy sequences and the final scene when Emmannuelle gives birth.

Contrary to the news headlines at the time, she never walked off the set – she was never anywhere near it, and her non-participation was amicable.

There are some nice touches in the casting. Susanne Danielle – later to become a regular on British television, in particular – is perfectly cast as the title character, managing to find an expressive performance in a poor script and the requirements of a 'comedy' French accent. However, Kenneth Williams gives his worst Carry On showing – a deeply uncomfortable performance: regular bit-part man Michael Nightingale gets two scenes and a fair amount of dialogue: Eric Barker returns as does Victor 'Milchmann' Maddern: Jack Douglas plays his part straight, and is good – as are Sims, Connor and Butterworth. Larry Dann is convincing – if irritating and a little manic – as the lovelorn Theadore, even if Beryl Reid, as his mother, looks like she would rather be elsewhere. However, the script remains a problem – neither funny enough, or toned down enough to meet a family audience via an 'A' certificate from the censor. Despite strenuous rewrites, an 'AA' certificate was issued, quite rightly, and the family audience – already jettisoned for *Carry On England* – was again inaccessible.

The Plot

- Wife of the French Ambassador in London (Kenneth Williams) – Emmannuelle (Suzanne Danielle) – comes to London to rekindle her relationship with her husband, for whom bodybuilding has become more interesting.
- On Concorde, she has a sexual encounter with the innocent Theodore Valentine (Larry Dann), who becomes obsessed with her and stalks her.
- Meanwhile, finding her husband unresponsive, she takes pleasure with high-ranking British officials, fearing that one may want to assassinate the Ambassador. The four members of the Ambassador's household (Joan Sims, Kenneth Connor, Peter Butterworth and Jack Douglas) tell tales of amorous encounters: in a wardrobe, during the war, at the zoo and in a launderette, while our heroine explains how the Ambassador came to lose his ardour after a sky-diving accident.
- Theodore visits a naked Emmannuelle and confesses his love. She rejects him. She visits bodybuilder Harry Hernia and Theadore follows in the hope of taking photographs and blackmailing her. She goes to a football match (Manchester United v Spurs, from the 'real' footage shown) and seduces various team members and the referee.
- Later, Theadore kidnaps her at gunpoint, and after she again rejects him, he exposes her as a sex maniac.
- She goes on television and does not deny or regret the allegations, describing an encounter with the Prime Minister. The Ambassador realises that his impotence is mental – not physical, and makes love to his wife, causing her

to become instantly faithful to him.

- After a revelation that he has been giving her fertility medication without her knowing, rather than anti-pregnancy pills, she gives birth surrounded by her friends – and lovers.

Analysis

'Misconceived and misspelled' quipped film journalist Derek Malcolm – referring to the second 'n' in *Emmannuelle*, and it is hard not to agree. Most of the subjects chosen for Carry On films – despite the commercial nature of the series – were universal, but in parodying something so transitory as the fashion for mainstream soft porn, *Carry On Emmannuelle* was destined to have a short life, and doomed the series to temporary oblivion. Indeed, there's a lot more about the film that sits poorly today than many of the other 1970s outings, and that's setting the bar pretty low. In an early, unfunny scene, she is questioned by Dino Shafeek, everyone's go-to comedy Indian in the 1970s. The joke is that the immigration officer is an Indian – and that's it. Another scene sees the Ambassador examined by an Indian Doctor, again a cringe-inducing, head-wobbling characterisation that really should have stayed in the 1970s.

Theodore's obsession is played for laughs, even though it is actually quite sinister. The final scene implies that her babies could be anyone's, even the football team are there. It is all rather unpleasant.

Overall, the jokes – where they come – are telegraphed and feel tacked on, and while the film is mostly harmless and moves along at quite a lick, it lacks consistent laughs and, as we have seen, its moral sensibilities are questionable. Although Connor, Sims, Butterworth and Douglas arc all good, the dialogue they are given is often embarrassing, and Williams should definitely have turned the part down, as his instincts told him to do.

The song that opens and closes the movie – 'Love Crazy' by Kenny Lynch (himself a multi-talented performer who endured racial stereotyping with a smile on his face throughout the 1970s) – is both irritatingly awful and annoyingly catchy. It might be the only part of the film the viewer remembers thirty minutes after seeing it.

While *Carry On Emmannuelle* is not quite as bad as *Carry On England*, it is nonetheless a shame that the main run of the series – this was number 30 – should end with such a poor, ill-conceived effort.

Carry On Columbus (1992)

Island World presents a Comedy House Production Executive
Produced by Peter Rogers
Produced by John Goldstone
Directed by Gerald Thomas
Screenplay by Dave Freeman (additional material from John Antrobus)
Director of Photography: Alan Hume
Music composed and conducted by John Du Prez.
Song 'Carry On Columbus' written and produced by Malcolm McLaren and Lee Gorman
Filming dates: Not known
UK release: 2 October 1992, US release: 20 November 1992
Running time: 91 minutes
Budget: £2,500,000

Cast:
Regulars: Jim Dale
Regular supporting cast: Jack Douglas, Leslie Phillips, Jon Pertwee, Peter Gilmore, June Whitfield
Guests: Bernard Cribbins, Maureen Lipman, Alexi Sayle, Rik Mayall, Sara Crowe, Julian Clary, Keith Allen, Richard Wilson, Rebecca Lacey, Nigel Planer, Larry Miller, Tony Slattery, Martin Clunes, Holly Aird, James Faulkner, Don Maclean, Daniel Peacock, Don Henderson, Charles Fleischer, Chris Langham, Peter Gordeno

As with 1984, when there had been a rush to release a film adaptation of 1984 by George Orwell, 1992 saw a rush of activity to mark 400 years of Columbus's discovery of the Americas. Two serious – and now pretty much forgotten – films were released in 1992 alongside *Carry On Columbus*. The Carry On film came about due to producer John Goldstone's interest in reviving the Hope/ Crosby *Road To...* films, with Gerald Thomas slated to direct and a succession of stars and writers attached. The plan remained in development for some time but segued into *Columbus* with the 400th anniversary looming. The script was handed over to Dave Freeman, a veteran writer but a man whose Carry On contributions – *Carry On Behind* and several of the *Carry On Laughing* TV shows – had hardly set the world alight.

The Plot

- Christopher Columbus (Jim Dale) persuades King Ferdinand (Leslie Phillips) and Queen Isabella (June Whitfield) to fund a trip to the East Indies with the hope of finding gold, despite the unwelcome attentions of the Spanish Inquisition. He recruits a motley crew, which includes his artist brother Bart (Peter Richardson) and navigator Mordecai (Bernard Cribbins), plus various volunteers and hardened criminals from Don Juan Diego's prison (Julian Clary).

- Meanwhile, the Turkish Sultan (Rik Mayall), fearing a new route would end his own lucrative trading route, dispatches Fatima (Sara Crowe) and Achmed (Alexi Sayle) to stop the voyage. After an incident where his crew accidentally destroys the ship of Countess Esmerelda (Maureen Lipman), Columbus is ordered to take her back to Spain. Defying orders, he heads east.
- Fatima falls in love with Columbus and abandons her plans of sabotage. Fed up with the bad food the crew mutiny, but just as he is to be hanged, Columbus and the crew spy land. It is America.
- The local natives – far cleverer than the new arrivals – fleece them. They dupe the crew into going into a booby-trapped mine and then send them packing with some pretend gold.
- Realising the deception on the way home, the crew stage a fake confiscation by the Inquisition, and set sail once again in search of real gold this time.

Analysis

The cast of the film is a rather uncomfortable hybrid of venerable comic talent, some of whom, like Bernard Cribbins and June Whitfield, had appeared in Carry On films previously, and many of the cast of the *Comic Strip* series of films, who had come to prominence during the 1980s on Channel 4. At the centre of the film – well cast, as it turned out – is Jim Dale, who thankfully had stayed in touch with Gerald Thomas.

With a desperately weak script to play with, however, which feels like someone writing a poor imitation of an innuendo-laden early 1970s Carry On outing, most of the cast struggle. Dale, for instance, gives an uneven performance, often on the verge of laughing in the middle of takes.

The Comic Strip actors, like Rik Mayall and Peter Richardson, seem completely out of place, mainly overacting wildly, although Keith Allen is convincingly menacing as Pepe the Poisoner. Julian Clary, on the other hand, displays no aptitude for acting at all, although a few of his caustic asides – his stock in trade – work better.

With a poor script, it requires an actor's craft to wring any humour available from the situation, and in this case it is down to Cribbins, Richard Wilson and Maureen Lipman to save whatever is left of the day. Of the younger performers, Sara Crowe – at that time a regular face in television comedy, and still acting today – gives an energetic and funny performance in the sort of role often given to Jacki Piper or Angela Douglas.

With only Jim Dale and Jack Douglas (in a small part) available to represent the regular cast from the 1970s, the film is littered with cameos from performers from the series in its heyday like Leslie Phillips, Peter Gilmore, June Whitfield and Jon Pertwee, and while it is great to see such much-loved performers alive and well, such a huge cast does not really aid the film.

Once the action moves to America, there is little improvement. That the natives (led by Charles Fleischer and Larry Miller) talk with New York accents is a nice touch to begin with, but this becomes irritating within a few minutes, and the plot continues to creak and groan, while the American performers seem as out of place as the Comic Strip cast – particularly Larry Miller.

The mine sequence – a parody of the Indiana Jones films – seems tacked on to lend a bit of action to the film, but like the other slapstick moments, seems laboured and cartoonish, barely raising a chuckle.

Watching the film, it is clear what Freeman was aiming at in his script. Many of the Carry On archetypes are there. Jim Dale is (bizarrely) Sid James, Sara Crowe is a hybrid of Barbara Windsor and Jacki Piper, Julian Clary is Charles Hawtrey and Richard Wilson is Kenneth Williams. Peter Richardson is Bernard Bresslaw, Bernard Cribbins is Kenneth Connor (as he was in *Jack* and *Spying*) and Maureen Lipman is Joan Sims or even June Whitfield in a film that already has June Whitfield in it. We desperately miss all those great stars, and if the point of *The Comic Strip* cast was to pass the torch to the new generation, it turns out that the new generation did not really want it in the first place.

Universally panned at the time of release, and to this day holding a rating of 3.0 on the Internet Movie Database (only *Emmannuelle* does worse at 2.9), it is very hard to find good things to say about *Columbus*. Yet the script does actually raise a few laughs, and Lipman, Wilson and Cribbins add a few that aren't really there through their class as performers. Dale, too, has a few moments, including the 'interrupted hanging' and a tongue-twisting exchange with Wilson. Yet overall, this is mainly laugh-free fare, and hard going even as a curiosity watch.

Carry On, On Television

Given its popularity, it was inevitable that the Carry On series should make the transition to television, but the move was not always an easy one. Possibly the most watchable remains the *What A Carry On* series of 30-minute compilations from 1984, which packages scenes from most of the films into short narrative sections. 13 episodes were compiled, and they were still shown regularly up until recently. However, it is also worth a decent look at the four Christmas specials made between 1969 and 1973.

Seventeen episodes of original television were shot by the team between 1969 and 1975, the partially successful (artistically at least) *Carry On Christmas* specials from 1969 to 1973 and the lamentable *Carry On Laughing* series in 1975. It is quite hard to pin down the precise reasons for the rather rough transition, though it is most likely that this stems from a perceived need to fit in with the conventions of British television at the start of the 1970s. On top of that, while there were always links between the series and the British Pantomime and music hall traditions, the presence of a studio audience and the seasonal nature of the broadcasts made this link even more obvious. While the films had become somewhat sexualised by this time, the TV specials took a slightly different tack, tapping into the tropes of the time– for instance poking fun at homosexuality – and there are a few jokes based around rape that have worn very badly, and with good reason.

Furthermore, there's a feeling of looseness and lack of rehearsal at times that seems a million miles away from the precision of the films, even the bad ones, and with the ubiquitous mixture of studio and canned laughter seeming a hindrance rather than a help, these Christmas specials have not worn particularly well in comparison to the films. While it can be fun to see a cast member 'corpse' (or laugh accidentally) there's rather too much of this, here, with Peter Butterworth a particular culprit.

Yet at the time – when there were only three TV channels to choose from – the four Christmas specials all gained large viewing figures, even when shown as repeats, and within the conventions of the time, they offer undemanding and largely harmless entertainment. Those cast members that were largely consistent in the film series – especially Hattie Jacques and Joan Sims – acquit themselves remarkably well – and two of the team get the opportunity to show off their comedy 'chops' with a wider range of roles than they were ever allowed in the films – namely Bernard Bresslaw (never less than excellent) and newcomer Jack Douglas. To my mind, however, the standout is Kenneth Connor, who goes above and beyond the requirements of each role to bring a little extra each time. His performances are a master class in comic acting and timing, particularly given the relative weakness of the scripts he is faced with. Thankfully, almost all the regulars make appearances, although Kenneth Williams – whose presence would have been well suited to this sort of production – is a notable absentee, while the absence of Jim Dale is somewhat more understandable. The only ever-present is Barbara Windsor, who again was well suited to such broad material.

Overall, however, where the four Christmas specials and the 1975 television series fall down is an adherence to the tropes of much TV Comedy, especially on ITV, with its lazy, easy-watching scripts. At risk of sounding like a terrible television snob, very few half-hour ITV comedies have stood the test of time in the same way that *Dad's Army* and *Porridge* (to give only two examples) on the BBC have, and these Carry On programmes suffer in the same way. None of them demonstrates any of the wit that the best of the films have, which is a shame, but hardly a shock.

Carry On Christmas (1969)

Thames Television In association with / executive produced by Peter Rogers
Cast: Sid James, Terry Scott, Charles Hawtrey, Hattie Jacques, Barbara Windsor, Bernard Bresslaw, Peter Butterworth and Frankie Howerd.
Producer: Peter Eton Director: Ronnie Baxter
Producer / Comedy Consultant: Gerald Thomas
Screenplay by Talbot Rothwell
Shot at Teddington Studios

Largely thought of as the best of the four specials, this first outing – an early colour offering on ITV – builds a series of hit-and-miss sketches around the rough plot of *A Christmas Carol* by Charles Dickens – albeit with diversions via Frankenstein's laboratory and the sitting room of Elizabeth Barrett Browning (Hattie Jacques). Scrooge is played by Sid James, who largely dispenses with any sort of characterisation, and plays him as Sid's usual loveable rogue, rather than the usual grim miser.

There is one great moment – when Scrooge attempts to seduce the Ghost of Christmas Present (a giggling Barbara Windsor) – when all the chemistry they demonstrated in the films returns, lifting the production out of mediocrity for a few moments. However, other sequences – like a torturous dance routine with most of the male cast dressed as conventgirls – have not aged well. Nonetheless, all the cast have fun in a variety of roles, although the production is somewhat dominated by a typical turn from Frankie Howerd, who was also about to star in Talbot Rothwell's *Up Pompeii* TV series. His role as Robert Browning is largely an excuse to launch into his stand up routine. The final sequence – an actual pantomime with Babs as Cinders – is very nicely done, even though Howerd's second appearance – this time as the Fairy Godmother – isn't quite so successful.

Carry On Again Christmas (1970)

Thames Television in association with / executive produced by Peter Rogers
Cast: Sid James, Terry Scott, Charles Hawtrey, Kenneth Connor, Barbara Windsor, Bernard Bresslaw, Bob Todd, Wendy Richard
Script: Sid Colin and Dave Freeman
Executive Producer: Peter Eton

Producer / Director: Alan Tarrant
Comedy Consultant: Gerald Thomas Shot at Teddington Studios

For their second Christmas special, the team this time turned to *Treasure Island* by Robert Louis Stevenson as a source of inspiration with Sid James as Long John Silver, and Kenneth Connor excellent in his first appearance, despite his character being largely superfluous. Indeed the cast overall – including Terry Scott as Squire Trelawney and a superbly committed performance from TV regular Bob Todd as Ben Gunn – all raise their games as if performing a far, far better script. Despite a good start – with most of the cast appearing as Long John Silver all at once – this is almost unwatchable with the script failing to give the cast anything to work with, resulting in some desperate overplaying.

That it was shot in black and white did not help – although it is not quite clear whether this was down to a cost-saving measure or (more likely) a strike by ITV crew in December 1970.

Carry On Christmas (1972)

Thames Television in association with / executive produced by Peter Rogers
Cast: Hattie Jacques, Joan Sims, Barbara Windsor, Kenneth Connor, Peter Butterworth, Jack Douglas, Norman Rossington, Brian Oulton, Billy Cornelius, Valerie Leon, Valerie Stanton
Script: Talbot Rothwell and Dave Freeman
Producer: Gerald Thomas
Director: Ronnie Baxter
Shot at Teddington Studios

Within the context of the TV specials, the third outing – in 1972 – is a return to form, set around the Christmas dinner of 'The Pudding Club' – a Victorian dining club chaired by Kenneth Connor (with West Country accent). Some of the jokes are very like the Benny Hill Show – the entire female cast seem to be 'gagging for it' – but it does present an opportunity for some somewhat variable sketches and songs. Norman Rossington was drafted in at the last minute to replace Charles Hawtrey after another argument over billing.

The dinner room siege sequence from Carry On *Up The Khyber* is repeated in an amended – and less funny – form, and it is Jack Douglas – whether twitching or not – that raises the most laughs throughout, while the Napoleonic-era mystery sketch towards the end of the show is probably the strangest sequence of all the four episodes. The show finishes with another Pantomime, a rather more authentic stab than the 1969 effort and good fun, even if Norman Rossington's camp character isn't a patch on what Hawtrey might have made of it, and Barbara Windsor makes an excellent principal boy.

Although the 1972 outing isn't at all bad, tonally it lets the side down, with the most overtly sexual – and sexist – script of the four. Valerie Leon, for instance, has nothing to do except bend over. That said, I do hold a special place for it in my heart – I remember large chunks of it, having seen it in its repeat showing in December 1974 when I was twelve – yet now I can see that it probably deserves its place as the third best of the specials.

Carry On Christmas (1973)

Thames Television in association with / executive produced by Peter Rogers
Script: Talbot Rothwell
Producer: Gerald Thomas
Director: Ronald Fouracre
Shot at Teddington Studios
Cast: Sid James, Joan Sims, Barbara Windsor, Kenneth Connor, Peter Butterworth, Bernard Bresslaw, Jack Douglas, Julian Holloway, Laraine Humphreys

If the first three TV specials celebrated Christmas at all, it was as a time for lechery, greed and gluttony. The fourth instalment, broadcast on 24th December 1973, remembered that Christmas is also a time for peace and kindness, with a few moments of genuine heart. Not that it is all perfect. A 'schoolgirl' Barbara Windsor on 'Santa' Sid James' lap now appears more than a little uncomfortable, and the opening caveman sketch is far from impressive. 'The Country House, 1759' sequence is somewhat better, if anything due to the great fun that the cast are having with their roles, particularly Sims, Connor and Bresslaw, and the First World War sketch – a reworking of the Christmas Day 1914 coming-together of Allied and German troops – is also nicely judged.

Sid James introducing the commercial breaks – in the 1970s, there were only two breaks for advertisements in an hour-long ITV programme – is also a nice touch, as is James' ease in talking to the camera. The ballet dance sequence, which features the entire main cast except James – including the men in tutus – is a rather bizarre concoction and the final Robin Hood sketch – which might have been a Carry On film in its own right in different circumstances – is also a little weak. The final coda – with its goodwill message – is pleasant enough, and overall, while the show is not on a par with any but the weaker films, within the context of the made-for-TV specials and series, it stands up pretty well.

Carry On Laughing (1975)

Kenneth Williams did not do any Carry On-related television at all, except for introducing a compilation of the Christmas shows with Barbara Windsor in 1983, and he was again absent for *Carry On Laughing*. These were two series – one of six episodes, the other seven – of half-hour comedies with historical settings of various sorts recorded for ATV and broadcast during 1975. While most of the regulars appear at some point, the scripts for most of these shows are very weak, relying even more than the Christmas specials on 1970s ITV situation comedy conventions. Some of the 'gay' jokes in particular, as well as the implication, as Barbara Windsor's characters often do, that all women are 'desperate for it', have not stood the test of time. The performances are usually acceptable, with Kenneth Connor as consistent as always, and Jack Douglas – playing a variety of roles – really comes into his own, but the dialogue and the horrible canned laughter render these shows almost unwatchable. Should you wish to pile in, all the episodes are dotted around as extras within the excellent ITV boxed sets of the films.

Show List

Every episode was directed by Alan Tarrant and produced by Gerald Thomas.

The Prisoner Of Spenda

First broadcast: 4 January 1975, this is one of the better outings – a parody of the Prisoner of Zenda.
Script: Dave Freeman
Main Cast: Sid James, Barbara Windsor, Joan Sims, Jack Douglas, Kenneth Connor, Peter Butterworth

The Baron Outlook

First broadcast: 11 January 1975.
Script: Dave Freeman
Main Cast: Sid James, Barbara Windsor, Joan Sims, Kenneth Connor, Peter Butterworth

The Sobbing Cavalier

First broadcast: 18 January 1975. A tale of the English Civil War.
Script: Dave Freeman
Main Cast: Sid James, Barbara Windsor, Joan Sims, Jack Douglas, Peter Butterworth

Orgy And Bess.

First broadcast: 25 January 1975. With (if I'm honest) better writers at the helm, this Elizabethan tale with Hattie Jacques cast as the Virgin Queen is the best of the bunch.
Script: Barry Cryer and Dick Vosburgh
Main Cast: Sid James, Barbara Windsor, Hattie Jacques, Jack Douglas, Peter Butterworth

One In The Eye For Harold

First broadcast: 1 February 1975. A tale of the Battle of Hastings. It's dreadful.
Script: Lew Schwarz
Main Cast: Joan Sims, Kenneth Connor, Jack Douglas

The Nine Old Cobblers

First broadcast: 8 February 1975. This was the first of three parodies of the Lord Peter Wimsey detective novels – and the television series that starred Ian

Carmichael which ran from 1972 to 1975. It stars Jack Douglas as Lord Peter Flimsy. Tonally, these stories bear little relation to the Carry On series, coming across as rather unfunny extended sketches that might have been better suited to The Two Ronnies had the scripts been better.
Script: Dave Freeman
Main Cast: Joan Sims, Kenneth Connor, Jack Douglas, Peter Butterworth

Under The Round Table

First Broadcast 26 October 1975. The first of two scripts set at King Arthur's court, with Kenneth Connor as Arthur, Joan Sims as Guinevere and Peter Butterworth as Merlin.
Script: Lew Schwarz
Main Cast: Joan Sims, Kenneth Connor, Jack Douglas, Peter Butterworth, Bernard Bresslaw

The Case Of The Screaming Winkles

First Broadcast 2 November 1975. Lord Peter Flimsy, part two.
Script: Dave Freeman
Main Cast: Joan Sims, Kenneth Connor, Jack Douglas, Peter Butterworth

And In My Lady's Chamber

First Broadcast: 9 November 1975. The first of two pre-Great War-set stories.
Script: Lew Schwarz
Main Cast: Joan Sims, Kenneth Connor, Jack Douglas, Peter Butterworth, Bernard Bresslaw, Barbara Windsor

Short Knight, Long Daze

First Broadcast: 16 November 1975. Arthur Part Two.
Script: Lew Schwarz
Main Cast: Joan Sims, Kenneth Connor, Jack Douglas, Peter Butterworth, Bernard Bresslaw

The Case Of The Coughing Parrot

First Broadcast 23 November 1975. Lord Peter Flimsy, part three.
Script: Dave Freeman
Main Cast: Joan Sims, Kenneth Connor, Jack Douglas, Peter Butterworth

Who Needs Kitchener

First Broadcast: 30 November 1975. The second of the two pre-Great War-set stories.
Script: Lew Schwarz
Main Cast: Joan Sims, Kenneth Connor, Jack Douglas,.Bernard Bresslaw, Barbara Windsor

Lamp-Posts Of The Empire

First Broadcast: 7 December 1975. A tale of the search for Doctor Livingstone (Dr Pavingstone played by Bernard Bresslaw here)

Script: Lew Schwarz

Main Cast: Joan Sims, Kenneth Connor, Jack Douglas, Bernard Bresslaw, Barbara Windsor

Carry On, On Stage

Carry On London

Script by Talbot Rothwell, Dave Freeman and Eric Merriman
Cast: Sid James, Barbara Windsor, Kenneth Connor, Peter Butterworth, Bernard Bresslaw, Jack Douglas
Directed by Bill Robertson

There were three stage productions branded as Carry Ons. The first was *Carry On London*, which, after a short two-week preview run at the Birmingham Hippodrome, played at the Victoria Palace Theatre from October 1973 to March 1975. Very much in the 'review' format, the show included dancers and an orchestra, with the cast often performing two shows per day. The show also coincided with the shooting of *Carry On Dick*, and some episodes of *Carry On Laughing,* which included all six of the regulars in the show.

Carry On Laughing With The Slimming Factory

The stage face written by Sam Cree, author of *The Mating Game* starring Kenneth Connor, Liz Fraser, Peter Butterworth, Jack Douglas and Anne Aston ran for a season at the Royal Opera House, Scarborough in the summer of 1976.

Wot A Carry On In Blackpool

This was another summer season run, this time starring Barbara Windsor and Bernard Bresslaw with a script by Barry Cryer and Dick Vosburgh. Another variety show, its theme was the revival of old music hall numbers.

Epilogue

Life as a jobbing actor can be hard, and so many of the stars of the Carry On series died young. Many failed to reach their 70s, and even Gerald Thomas died at 73. While for many like Kenneth Williams and Joan Sims, the films offered a certain level of financial certainty, they never paid well enough for the actors to escape what was, by all accounts, nonetheless a very happy, if sometimes dysfunctional, working family.

There is little doubt that the series was a product of its time, and can never be repeated in quite the same way. The creators of the Carry Ons learned their craft from the popular culture of the 1920s, 1930s and 1940s: in radio comedy, in the latter days of the music hall, in local journalism and in the army concert party. Yet by the time they were making films themselves, the world was liberalising and they could bring more of their risqué vision to the screen. In the 1970s, they probably took this too far.

While the comedy of the 1980s reacted against the sexism and racism of British television (rather than the Carry On films specifically), the glorious – for want of a better word – 'silliness' of the Carry On series remains an influence on British comedy even now. It can be found in *The Comic Strip*, *The Young Ones, Blackadder,* and so many more, continuing into the 21st century. After all, who doesn't love a cringe-inducing pun?

Despite constant rumours of a revival, the deaths of Ian Lavender and – more crucially – Barbara Windsor and Bernard Cribbins mean that whatever happens, the cast and creators will have to be new. It won't be the same.

A planned revival to be produced by Peter Rogers called *Carry On London*, went as far as photoshoots during 2003. The cast was to include Shane Richie and Danniella Westbrook. The plot was to be based around a limousine company, Lenny's Limos. However, with production slipping into 2004 and beyond, most of the cast left, and Rogers' death in 2009 finally put paid to it for the time being.

In the final analysis, the Carry On series was good, clean, dirty fun, and – to borrow a phrase from the great Douglas Adams – it was 'mostly harmless'. What's wrong with that?

Bibliography And Further Information

Webber, R., 50 Years of Carry On (Arrow Books, 2008)
Snelgrove,K., Hume, A., The Original Carry On Facts, Figures and Statistics (Apex Publishing, 2016)
Ross, A., Carry On Actors: The Complete Who's Who of the Carry On Series (Fantom Films, 2015)
Ed. Davies, R., The Kenneth Williams Diaries (Harper Collins, 1994)

The 30 Carry On films up to *Emmannuelle* are owned by ITV and available as a boxed set. Originally released in the early 2000s, the set includes director's commentaries on all 30 films, conducted by Carry On historian Richard Ross with members of the original casts, and occasionally Peter Rogers. Some of the participants are no longer with us, including Peter Rogers himself and Terence Longdon. All thirteen episodes of the *Carry On Laughing* television series are also included, dotted around the boxed sets.

The films are also available in four-film DVD sets, and can also be viewed via Amazon video on a pay-per-view basis.

The four Christmas Shows are available as a separate DVD boxed set, with a variety of extras including interviews and a special Evening with Peter Rogers.

Should you wish to see *Carry On Columbus* it is available separately on DVD via Warner Home Entertainment.

Carry On Forever is a three-part television documentary series made for ITV by independent production company Shiver. It was first broadcast in the spring of 2015 and repeated in 2018. Each part looks at an 'era' of about ten films, and includes interviews with many of the stars still with us. Narrated by actor Martin Clunes (who was in *Columbus*), the tone is celebratory and somewhat sentimental, with (for instance) Patrick Mower visiting the anti-aircraft gun used in *England* at the Imperial War Museum, and Angela Douglas visiting the *Up The Khyber* sets in Snowdonia. Nonetheless, for Carry On fans this is an essential watch.

Appendices

1: Oh I Do Feel Queer! Carry On Tropes In The Talbot Rothwell Era

Given that he wrote over twenty stories for the Carry On films, it is inevitable that certain themes crop up again and again in his scripts. Some of these – like the constant usage of catchphrases, for instance – are obvious, as is a comedic obsession with breasts. However, many of these only become apparent when watching many films in the series over a short period. Here are six that readers may want to look out for. There are probably many more.

Large Groups Of Women As Objects Of Fantasy

I place this first as it is an astonishing feature of almost every Rothwell script.

Somewhere, there is a large group of women that bewitch a smaller group of men. As far back as *Cabby* we have the Glamcab drivers lined up in a row, but there are many others.

The all-female, high-booted staff of S.T.E.N.C.H in *Spying*, the Vestal Virgins in *Cleo*, the dancing girls in *Cowboy*, the Harem in *Follow That Camel*, the Khasi's wives and the 'hospitality girls' in *Khyber*, the Lubidubies in *Up The Jungle*, the Birds of Paradise in *Dick* and many more. This may simply be intentional titillation for the male viewer, of course, and it would be wrong of me to suggest that Rothwell (or indeed Rogers or Thomas) had a 'thing' about large groups of semi-clad beautiful women without any evidence, but there really are a lot of them.

Readers can judge for themselves.

Cross Dressing

This has a great tradition in the theatre, of course, harking back to the pantomime dame and principal boy, not to mention the British Forces concert party. In that tradition, Talbot does love to dress his men as women in almost every film. In particular, due to his square, masculine face, he seems to love putting Peter Butterworth in ladies' clothes for comic effect (see *Screaming* and *Follow That Camel*). Who was the most convincing? Probably Jim Dale in *Spying*. The least convincing? Almost everyone else – do you remember Sid James in *Don't Lose Your Head*, *At Your Convenience* and *Dick*? There are others: Charles Hawtrey in *Again Doctor*, Kenneth Cope in *Matron* and Bernard Bresslaw in *Doctor* and *Girls*. In all these films, the plot requires the person dressed up to be convincing, if only for a short while, when the viewer knows that they are anything but. This is false subterfuge of Shakespearean quality.

The cross-dressing does go the other way occasionally, albeit less frequently. Angela Douglas wears a cowboy outfit towards the end of *Cowboy*, Juliet Mills spends most of *Jack* in a naval uniform and Barbara Windsor dresses as a man in *Dick*, before being 'uncovered' in somewhat explicit fashion.

Hints At The Homosexuality Of Kenneth Williams And Charles Hawtrey

While they were both practising homosexuals (although Williams spent large parts of his life celibate), both actors usually played camp but robustly heterosexual men in the Carry On films. Williams' characters are usually frightened or inexperienced, while Hawtrey's are rather more rampant.

In *Doctor*, while the advances of Hattie Jacques' Matron terrify him, there is a suggestion that Tinkle (Williams) may have sexually exploited Barbara Windsor's May. In *Don't Lose Your Head*, *Henry* and *Khyber* Hawtrey's characters are almost aggressively heterosexual. However, several of Rothwell's scripts contain unsubtle references to their sexuality. Significantly, some of these scripts pre-dated the legalisation of homosexuality in 1967, and maybe knowing declarations of defiance on the part of the cast. In *Cleo* Kenneth Williams as Caesar says, at one point early in the film 'Oh, I do feel queer', while Hawtrey and Joan Sims have a similar exchange in *Henry* – just before his character goes on to father her child.

> Hawtrey: Oh, I can be a one when I want
> Sims: Yes, I thought you might be one.

Although a lonely character in his private life, Williams also did much to popularise gay culture in the radio series *Round The Horn* in conjunction with Hugh Paddick and their characters Julian and Sandy. Hawtrey, however, was rather more obvious in his sexuality, albeit as circumspect as he needed to be prior to 1967.

Right-Wing Sentiments

Norman Hudis was a writer with rather progressive views, leading ultimately to the rejection of his script for *Spying*, which featured an anti-nuclear theme. Rothwell, on the other hand, was understandably vilified for his stab at the trade unions in *At Your Convenience,* and generally his scripts fit in rather better with the conservative (with a small c) attitudes of Rogers and Thomas. Objectifying women – a key feature of the series – clearly came easily to him, but so did little digs at the supposed laziness of the British working classes. These are thrown in all over the series, but as early as *Cabby,* we have a character that is a Union representative (played by Norman Mitchell) whose views are used for comic effect rather than taken seriously. In context, therefore, his script for *At Your Convenience* was not quite the shock it might have been.

The 'Blooming' Of Supposedly Unattractive Women

The dowdy secretary who takes off her glasses and shakes out her hair in slow-motion to reveal that she is, in fact, beautiful, is a traditional fantasy of heterosexual men, and a much-loved device of Talbot Rothwell. As with his use of unconvincing men in drag, in all these cases, the plot requires us to assume these women are unattractive before their transformation. In *Up The Jungle*, Sid James attempts to seduce Jacki Piper as an act of desperation, but without the glasses that she suddenly no longer needs, she finds happiness with the Jungle Boy Cecil (Terry Scott). In both *Loving* and *Girls*, dowdy women (Imogen Hassall and Valerie Leon, respectively) become immediately more desirable – and, for some reason, suddenly more promiscuous as characters – when they dress sexily.

Speeded-Up Film

Given the very physical nature of much of the comedy, it is hardly surprising that the series should use devices common to silent film and even cartoons. Film is often sped up in the 1960s Rothwell films, though this device was used less from the late 1960s onwards. There are two reasons for this.

Firstly, it is used for pacing. In the climax of *Spying,* for instance, our heroes travel through Dr. Crow's machinery at normal speed, but when the process is reversed, they travel back much more quickly, since it would be tedious to see the entire process reversed at normal pace, as well as revealing even more clearly that the editor has just played the film backwards. In *At Your Convenience*, a rare later usage of this device, sped-up film is used on the journey home after the works outing to give an impression of repetition as the coach repeatedly stops. In this case, the music is sped up as well.

Often, however, this device is used to cover up less-than-impressive physical jokes and special effects. In the climactic fight sequence that closes *Don't Lose Your Head,* Sid James slides down a bannister. The camera is sped up to disguise, one suspects, a rather slow descent in reality. Later in the same sequence, Charles Hawtrey (or rather a stuntman disguised as him) swings through a window in spectacular fashion, but the film is sped up to make it seem more spectacular than it probably was.

2: Gaw, blimey! The Carry On Love Life Of Sid James

From the Rothwell period onwards, Sid James' screen persona was pretty much consistent. With his 'conventional' romantic leading man role in *Don't Lose Your Head,* a slightly uncomfortable exception, the Sid we all came to know and love was a lovable lecher, generally in a relationship with one woman, while lusting after a much younger one. Most often, however, he sees the error of his ways by the end of the film, and realises that the woman he has spurned is the one for him. Usually, but not always, Sid is married to Joan Sims and lusts after Barbara Windsor, most notably in *Carry On Abroad.* His relationships are most realistic, however, in *Carry On Loving*, where we find him in a long-term relationship with Hattie Jacques, while lusting after Joan Sims, repeated in *At Your Convenience,* but with rather more tenderness, unusual for a Rothwell script. Here are all his relationships across each of his nineteen appearances:

Constable – Hint at a potential relationship with Hattie Jacques.
Regardless – None, unless you consider his secretary, Esma Cannon, which you probably can't.
Cruising – None, but fancied briefly by Dilys Laye.
Cabby – Married to Hattie Jacques, married also to his business.
Cleo – Lusts after – and wins – Amanda Barrie.
Cowboy – Fancies Joan Sims, then Angela Douglas. Ends up with Sims.
Don't Lose Your Head – Falls for Dany Robin, fancied by Joan Sims.
Doctor – Married to Dandy Nicholls.
Up The Khyber – Married to Joan Sims, has 'tiffin' with thirteen of the Khasi's wives.
Camping – In a relationship with Joan Sims, fancies Barbara Windsor, ends up with Sims.
Again Doctor – Seven wives including Patsy Rowlands. Fancies Hattie Jacques (briefly).
Up The Jungle – Fancies Jacki Piper as a last resort and some of the Lubidubi tribe.
Loving – In a relationship with Hattie Jacques, fancies Joan Sims.
Henry – Married to Joan Sims, fancies Barbara Windsor.
At Your Convenience – Married to Hattie Jacques, loves Joan Sims.
Matron – Married unsuccessfully to crime.
Abroad – Married to Joan Sims, fancies Barbara Windsor, stays with Sims.
Girls – In a relationship with Joan Sims, fancies and wins Barbara Windsor.
Dick – In a relationship with God, fancies and wins Barbara Windsor, loved by Hattie Jacques.

3: The Carry On Roll Of Honour (Or, Who On Earth Is Michael Nightingale?)

Many actors made more than one appearance in the Carry On series. This list shows all of them in order of the number of films they appeared in. I include *That's Carry On,* but only its two presenters – Kenneth Williams and Barbara Windsor. A few things jump out immediately when looking down the list.

Firstly, despite having notched up several appearances, Barbara Windsor – one of the actors most associated with the series – did not become a regular until 1972, when it could be argued that the Carry Ons were in decline.

Secondly, three actors stand out for the frequency of their supporting roles. The wonderful character actress Marianne Stone notched up over 250 appearances in a career that began in 1943 and ended in 1989. Amazingly, most (but not all) of these were in film rather than TV. Although she is best known for her eleven appearances in the Carry Ons (one of which, in *Constable,* was just a dubbed voice over) and a twelfth – *Matron* – where her scenes did not make the final cut – she was in many of the most iconic British films of the post war period including *Brighton Rock, A Night To Remember* and *Lolita.*

After appearing in eleven Carry On films, the hugely versatile actor Peter Gilmore found real fame playing shipping company owner James Onedin in the early 1970s series *The Onedin Line.* After starring in that series, which ran for nine years from 1971 to 1980, he felt himself to be typecast. Not so, however, in the Carry Ons where his roles included: Robespierre in *Don't Lose Your Head*, the King of France in *Henry* and a *Doctor* in *Again Doctor.* His best-known scene has him playing an ambulance driver outside a hospital in *Doctor*, and has Barbara Windsor admiring the quality of the pear he is eating. You probably know the one.

Although not quite as ubiquitous in British film and television as Marianne Stone, Michael Nightingale was a regular character actor from the late 1940s onwards. He notched up thirteen appearances in the series, usually playing a city gent or minor authority figure. A great favourite of Rogers and Thomas, his early appearances were little more than walk-ons, but towards the end of the series, they were giving him featured scenes. He plays the Doctor in *Matron* that examines Kenneth Williams, Squire Trelawny in *Dick* and the Police Commissioner in *Emmannuelle.*

The Roll Of Honour

Kenneth Williams – 26
Charles Hawtrey – 24
Joan Sims – 24
Sid James – 19
Kenneth Connor – 17
Peter Butterworth – 16
Bernard Bresslaw – 14
Hattie Jacques – 14
Michael Nightingale – 13
Marianne Stone – 11
Jim Dale – 11
Peter Gilmore – 11
Barbara Windsor – 10
Patsy Rowlands – 9
Jack Douglas – 8
Terry Scott – 8
Julian Holloway – 8
Cyril Chamberlain – 8
Derek Francis – 8
Frank Forsyth- 8
Anthony Sagar – 7
Billy Cornelius – 6
Brian Osborne – 6
Gertan Klauber – 6
Hugh Fulcher – 6
Ian Wilson – 6
Lucy Griffiths – 6
Margaret Nolan – 6
Valerie Leon – 6
Bill Maynard -5
David Lodge – 5
Joan Hickson – 5
Victor Maddern – 5
Amelia Bayntun – 5
Michael Ward – 5
Norman Mitchell – 5
Patricia Franklin – 5
Patrick Durkin – 5
Sally Douglas – 5
Tom Clegg – 5
Angela Douglas – 4
Jacki Piper – 4
June Whitfield – 4
Leslie Phillips – 4
Liz Fraser – 4
Bill Owen – 4
Brian Oulton – 4
Eric Barker – 4
Jon Pertwee – 4
Larry Dann – 4
Terence Longdon – 4
Dilys Laye – 4
Dominique Don – 4
Ed Devereaux – 4
Esma Cannon – 4
Julian Orchard – 4
Marian Collins – 4
Valerie Van Ost – 4
Bernard Cribbins – 3
John Bluthal – 3
Kenneth Cope – 3
Norman Rossington – 3
Sally Geeson – 3
Shirley Eaton – 3
Renée Houston – 3
Amanda Barrie – 2
Anita Harris – 2
Betty Marsden – 2
Carol Hawkins – 2
Diane Langton – 2
Fenella Fielding – 2
Frankie Howerd – 2
Jimmy Logan – 2
Peter Jones – 2
Richard O'Callaghan – 2
Rosalind Knight – 2
Windsor Davies – 2
June Jago – 2
Percy Herbert – 2

4: The Ones That Got Away: Carry On Films That Were Never Made And Related Films That Were...

The Ones That Got Away

Peter Rogers had many ideas that never got off the ground. Sometimes – as with *Carry On Robin* – to be about Robin Hood and later to become a sketch in one of the Christmas specials – he merely registered the title with the British Film Producers Association but never pursued it. Others were discussed repeatedly and even went into pre-production. *Carry On Spaceman* – about the space race – was nearly made twice in the early 1960s with scripts by Norman Hudis on both occasions.

Talbot Rothwell wrote a complete script for *Carry On Escaping* in 1973, but the film never made it into production. Two films were planned for the early 1980s – *Carry On Dallas* had a completed script, but production was cancelled after Lorimar Productions – the makers of the hugely popular glossy soap opera *Dallas* – demanded a royalty twenty times the size of the film's budget. *Carry On Down Under* was also planned after Gerald Thomas scouted locations when on holiday in Australia. A script was written by Vince Powell, but the film was abandoned when financing fell through.

The most torturous story of what might have been, however, belongs to *Carry On Again Nurse*, which was registered by Rogers as early as the 1960s. The first attempt was renamed *Carry On Doctor* and released in 1968. A second script was written by comedy writers Jonathan Lynn (who went on to write *Yes Minister*) and George Layton (who played the doctor in *Behind*) in 1977, but was never filmed following the poor box-office performance of *Emmannuelle*. The final attempt was to be the first proper revival of the series, to be filmed in 1988. Written by Norman Hudis, the film was to have starred most of the regulars that were still alive, including Kenneth Williams, Charles Hawtrey, Barbara Windsor, Jack Douglas and Joan Sims (who would have played Matron), but was cancelled after the deaths of Williams and Hawtrey, and an escalating budget made it unfeasible.

Closely Related Films

Carry On Admiral (1957 – also known as *The Ship Was Loaded*)

This naval comedy starring David Tomlinson was written and directed by Val Guest, a veteran of the British screen, particularly in comedy, having worked since the 1930s with stars like Will Hay. This particular film, shot at Elstree, has a coincidental title, a light tone and – in Joan Sims and Joan Hickson – two actresses who would later appear in the Carry On series. The film failed to make a great deal of impact at the box office, even when re-released in the wake of the success of *Carry On Sergeant*.

Please Turn Over (1959)

A light comedy about a teenager who writes a steamy bestseller based on the lives of her family and community, produced by Peter Rogers, directed by

Gerald Thomas and written by Norman Hudis. It stars Ted Ray, Leslie Phillips and Joan Sims, amongst others, as well as Charles Hawtrey and Dilys Laye in smaller roles.

Watch Your Stern (1960)

Another naval comedy from the Peter Rogers / Gerald Thomas partnership, this time with an even bigger cast of Carry On regulars, including main character Kenneth Connor plus Eric Barker, Leslie Phillips, Joan Sims (again), Hattie Jacques and Sid James.

Raising The Wind (1961 – also known as *Roommates*)

Another Rogers/Thomas comedy, about some musical students sharing a house, this film is cast almost as if it were a Carry On with parts for Kenneth Williams, Sid James, Leslie Phillips, Eric Barker and Esma Cannon, although, amazingly, no role for Joan Sims.

Twice Round The Daffodils (1962)

The 'cousin' of *Carry On Nurse*, this comedic drama was based on the play *Ring For Catty* by Patrick Cargill and Jack Beale, the play which had also inspired *Nurse*. Again produced by Rogers, directed by Thomas and with a script by Hudis, the film's main character was played by Juliet Mills, with parts also for Donald Houston, like Mills to appear in *Carry On Jack* the following year, plus Joan Sims and Kenneth Williams.

Nurse On Wheels (1963)

Although not part of the Carry On series, this breezy and successful comedy starring Juliet Mills as a district nurse was marketed heavily on the reputation of the series. Again, a product of the Thomas / Rogers / Hudis axis, there were parts for Joan Sims (of course), Esma Cannon and Jim Dale.

The Big Job (1965)

Starring Sid James, Joan Sims (of course) and Jim Dale from the Carry On stable, this successful caper comedy, written by Talbot Rothwell and directed by Gerald Thomas, with Peter Rogers producing, also featured the talents of Dick Emery and Sylvia Syms, as well as a myriad of other supporting actors with Carry On credentials.

Bless This House (1972)

By the mid-1960s, Peter Rogers was concentrating on the punishing twice-yearly Carry On Schedule, but with one exception. *Bless This House* was a hugely popular ITV situation comedy series which ran for six series between 1971 and 1976. A vehicle for Sid James, based largely on generation gap issues, the series also starred Sally Geeson as his daughter. As with many popular sitcoms of the time, the series had one big-screen outing via Peter Rogers Productions, with

Gerald Thomas directing and a script by Dave Freeman. There were two major casting changes from the TV series, with Robin Asquith playing Mike, Sid's son, and Peter Butterworth taking over the part of next-door neighbour Trevor. However, the supporting cast reads like a Carry On 'who's who' with Terry Scott and June Whitfield playing husband and wife, but also Patsy Rowlands (who was also in the sitcom), Carol Hawkins, Bill Maynard, Marianne Stone, Julian Orchard, Patricia Franklin and even old hand Ed Devereux involved.

5: The Carry Ons - Rated In Order From 1 To 30

How would you grade the Carry On series in terms of quality? Here's how the author feels about them. In truth, I'd watch any of the 31 films again in a heartbeat and, as I have pointed out already, there are things even in *Emmannuelle* and *Columbus* that I like, but give me *Cowboy* or *Cleo* any day of the week.

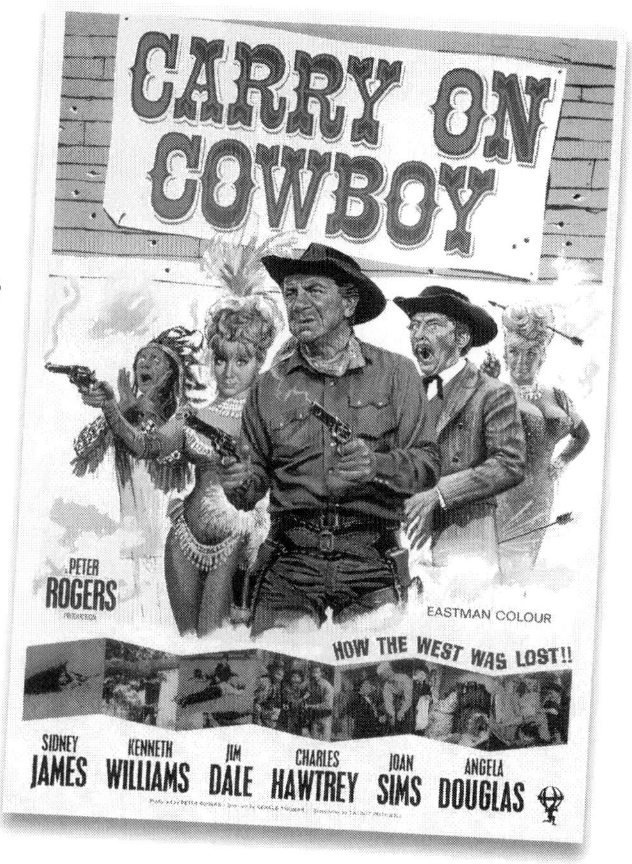

The Classics

Cowboy
Cleo
Khyber
Spying
Abroad
Cabby

The Best Of The Rest

Doctor
Don't Lose Your Head
Regardless
Screaming
Constable
Girls
Camping
Cruising

Decent Efforts

Teacher
Nurse
Sergeant
Again Doctor
Follow That Camel
Loving
Jack

Passable On A Wet Sunday Afternoon

Henry
Matron
Up The Jungle
Dick
At Your Convenience
Behind

The Really Poor Ones

England
Emmannuelle
Columbus

6: Best Carry On Performances

This is where to find the regular actors' best performances, in the humble opinion of your author, of course...

Kenneth Williams

His Caesar in *Cleo* balances the camp with comedy perfectly, but also try *Sergeant* for some actual, bona fide dramatic acting!

Charles Hawtrey

His pitch-perfect cameo in *Screaming* is wonderful, but I also love him for his opening greeting in *Constable*.

Joan Sims

Her early performance in *Teacher* demonstrates what a good comic actress she was, but also *Up The Khyber* shows off the passion that lay within.

Sid James

Again Doctor, though not his largest part, shows Sid at his exuberant best but he's great in almost everything, try *Constable* for a more conventional performance.

Kenneth Connor

Regardless shows off his true virtuosity as a comedic actor, he is the funniest thing in the film, but he's also great in *Cleo*.

Peter Butterworth

Who can forget his performance in the climactic final siege in *Up The Khyber*, but for a cameo, I recommend his magnificent scene in *Again Doctor*.

Bernard Bresslaw

Although best known for his gormless nice guy roles, best shown in *Doctor* his terrifying ethnic warriors were also a sight to behold, particularly in *Follow That Camel*.

Hattie Jacques

Hattie was not best served by all those Matron roles, where her best performance can be found in *Nurse*. However, her best Carry On performance by far is as the sympathetic, neglected wife in *Cabby*.

Jim Dale

Cowboy is the film that saw Jim Dale really get noticed, a performance of huge energy and comic timing, repeated beautifully in *Follow That Camel*.

Barbara Windsor

Girls is where Babs gets the balance between sexiness and cheekiness just right, though she is also excellent in *Again Doctor*.

Terry Scott

Camping shows Terry at his most sympathetic, although his best performance may just be as the shouty sergeant in *Up The Khyber*.

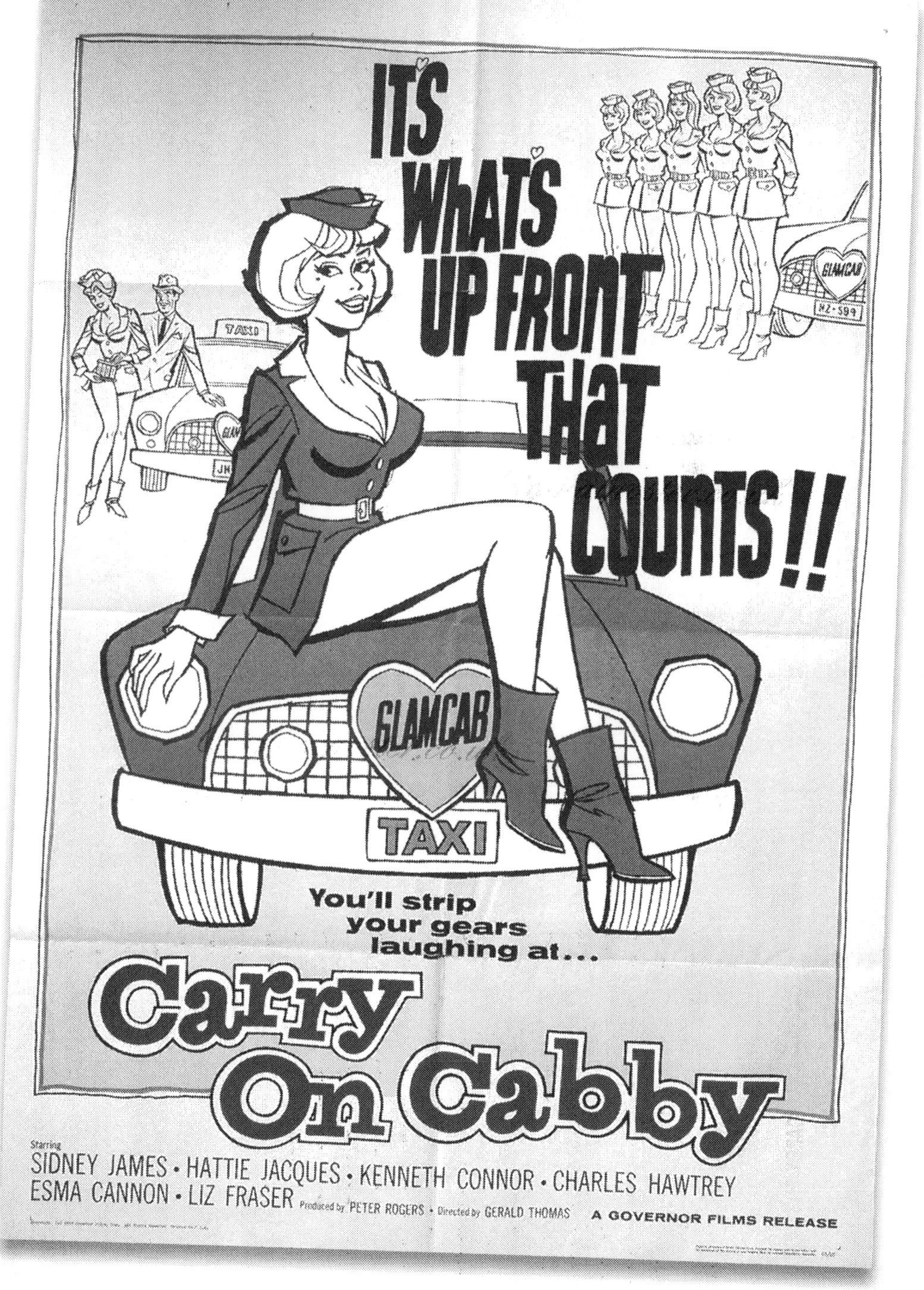
IT'S WHAT'S UP FRONT THAT COUNTS!!
TAXI
GLAMCAB
HZ-599
GLAMCAB
TAXI
You'll strip your gears laughing at...
Carry On Cabby
Starring
SIDNEY JAMES • HATTIE JACQUES • KENNETH CONNOR • CHARLES HAWTREY
ESMA CANNON • LIZ FRASER Produced by PETER ROGERS • Directed by GERALD THOMAS
A GOVERNOR FILMS RELEASE

Also available from Sonicbond

On Track series

AC/DC – Chris Sutton 978-1-78952-307-2
Allman Brothers Band – Andrew Wild 978-1-78952-252-5
Tori Amos – Lisa Torem 978-1-78952-142-9
Aphex Twin – Beau Waddell 978-1-78952-267-9
Asia – Peter Braidis 978-1-78952-099-6
Badfinger – Robert Day-Webb 978-1-878952-176-4
Barclay James Harvest – Keith and Monica Domone 978-1-78952-067-5
Beck – Arthur Lizie 978-1-78952-258-7
The Beat, General Public, Fine Young Cannibals – Steve Parry 978-1-78952-274-7
The Beatles 1962-1996 – Alberto Bravin and Andrew Wild 978-1-78952-355-3
The Beatles Solo 1969-1980 – Andrew Wild 978-1-78952-030-9
Blue Oyster Cult – Jacob Holm-Lupo 978-1-78952-007-1
Blur – Matt Bishop 978-178952-164-1
Marc Bolan and T.Rex – Peter Gallagher 978-1-78952-124-5
David Bowie 1964 to 1982 – Carl Ewens 978-1-78952-324-9
David Bowie 1963 to 2016 – Don Klees 978-1-78952-351-5
Kate Bush – Bill Thomas 978-1-78952-097-2
The Byrds – Andy McArthur 978-1-78952-280-8
Camel – Hamish Kuzminski 978-1-78952-040-8
Captain Beefheart – Opher Goodwin 978-1-78952-235-8
Caravan – Andy Boot 978-1-78952-127-6
Cardiacs – Eric Benac 978-1-78952-131-3
Wendy Carlos – Mark Marrington 978-1-78952-331-7
The Carpenters – Paul Tornbohm 978-1-78952-301-0
Nick Cave and The Bad Seeds – Dominic Sanderson 978-1-78952-240-2
Eric Clapton Solo – Andrew Wild 978-1-78952-141-2
The Clash (revised edition) – Nick Assirati 978-1-78952-325-6
Elvis Costello and The Attractions – Georg Purvis 978-1-78952-129-0
Crosby, Stills and Nash – Andrew Wild 978-1-78952-039-2
Creedence Clearwater Revival – Tony Thompson 978-1-78952-237-2
Crowded House – Jon Magidsohn 978-1-78952-292-1
The Damned – Morgan Brown 978-1-78952-136-8
David Bowie 1964 to 1982 – Carl Ewens 978-1-78952-324-9
David Bowie 1964 to 1982 – Carl Ewens 978-1-78952-324-9
Deep Purple and Rainbow 1968-79 – Steve Pilkington 978-1-78952-002-6
Deep Purple from 1984 – Phil Kafcaloudes 978-1-78952-354-6
Depeche Mode – Brian J. Robb 978-1-78952-277-8
Dire Straits – Andrew Wild 978-1-78952-044-6
The Divine Comedy – Alan Draper 978-1-78952-308-9
The Doors – Tony Thompson 978-1-78952-137-5
Dream Theater – Jordan Blum 978-1-78952-050-7

Bob Dylan 1962-1970 – Opher Goodwin 978-1-78952-275-2
Eagles – John Van der Kiste 978-1-78952-260-0
Earth, Wind and Fire – Bud Wilkins 978-1-78952-272-3
Electric Light Orchestra – Barry Delve 978-1-78952-152-8
Emerson Lake and Palmer – Mike Goode 978-1-78952-000-2
Fairport Convention – Kevan Furbank 978-1-78952-051-4
Peter Gabriel – Graeme Scarfe 978-1-78952-138-2
Genesis – Stuart MacFarlane 978-1-78952-005-7
Gentle Giant – Gary Steel 978-1-78952-058-3
Gong – Kevan Furbank 978-1-78952-082-8
Green Day – William E. Spevack 978-1-78952-261-7
Steve Hackett – Geoffrey Feakes 978-1-78952-098-9
Hall and Oates – Ian Abrahams 978-1-78952-167-2
Peter Hammill – Richard Rees Jones 978-1-78952-163-4
Roy Harper – Opher Goodwin 978-1-78952-130-6
Hawkwind (new edition) – Duncan Harris 978-1-78952-290-7
Jimi Hendrix – Emma Stott 978-1-78952-175-7
The Hollies – Andrew Darlington 978-1-78952-159-7
Horslips – Richard James 978-1-78952-263-1
The Human League and The Sheffield Scene – Andrew Darlington 978-1-78952-186-3
Humble Pie –Robert Day-Webb 978-1-78952-2761
Ian Hunter – G. Mick Smith 978-1-78952-304-1
The Incredible String Band – Tim Moon 978-1-78952-107-8
INXS – Manny Grillo 978-1-78952-302-7
Iron Maiden – Steve Pilkington 978-1-78952-061-3
Joe Jackson – Richard James 978-1-78952-189-4
The Jam – Stan Jeffries 978-1-78952-299-0
Jefferson Airplane – Richard Butterworth 978-1-78952-143-6
Jethro Tull – Jordan Blum 978-1-78952-016-3
J. Geils Band – James Romag 978-1-78952-332-4
Elton John in the 1970s – Peter Kearns 978-1-78952-034-7
Billy Joel – Lisa Torem 978-1-78952-183-2
Journey – Doug Thornton 978-1-78952-337-9
Judas Priest – John Tucker 978-1-78952-018-7
Kansas – Kevin Cummings 978-1-78952-057-6
Killing Joke – Nic Ransome 978-1-78952-273-0
The Kinks – Martin Hutchinson 978-1-78952-172-6
Korn – Matt Karpe 978-1-78952-153-5
Led Zeppelin – Steve Pilkington 978-1-78952-151-1
Level 42 – Matt Philips 978-1-78952-102-3
Little Feat – Georg Purvis – 978-1-78952-168-9
Magnum – Matthew Taylor – 978-1-78952-286-0

Also available from Sonicbond

Aimee Mann – Jez Rowden 978-1-78952-036-1
Ralph McTell – Paul O. Jenkins 978-1-78952-294-5
Metallica – Barry Wood 978-1-78952-269-3
Joni Mitchell – Peter Kearns 978-1-78952-081-1
The Moody Blues – Geoffrey Feakes 978-1-78952-042-2
Motorhead – Duncan Harris 978-1-78952-173-3
Nektar – Scott Meze – 978-1-78952-257-0
New Order – Dennis Remmer – 978-1-78952-249-5
Nightwish – Simon McMurdo – 978-1-78952-270-9
Nirvana – William E. Spevack 978-1-78952-318-8
Laura Nyro – Philip Ward 978-1-78952-182-5
Oasis – Andrew Rooney 978-1-78952-300-3
Phil Ochs – Opher Goodwin 978-1-78952-326-3
Mike Oldfield – Ryan Yard 978-1-78952-060-6
Opeth – Jordan Blum 978-1-78-952-166-5
Pearl Jam – Ben L. Connor 978-1-78952-188-7
Tom Petty – Richard James 978-1-78952-128-3
Pink Floyd – Richard Butterworth 978-1-78952-242-6
The Police – Pete Braidis 978-1-78952-158-0
Porcupine Tree (Revised Edition) – Nick Holmes 978-1-78952-346-1
Procol Harum – Scott Meze 978-1-78952-315-7
Queen – Andrew Wild 978-1-78952-003-3
Radiohead – William Allen 978-1-78952-149-8
Gerry Rafferty – John Van der Kiste 978-1-78952-349-2
Rancid – Paul Matts 978-1-78952-187-0
Lou Reed 1972-1986 – Ethan Roy 978-1-78952-283-9
Renaissance – David Detmer 978-1-78952-062-0
REO Speedwagon – Jim Romag 978-1-78952-262-4
The Rolling Stones 1963-80 – Steve Pilkington 978-1-78952-017-0
Linda Ronstadt 1969-1989 – Daryl O. Lawrence 987-1-78952-293-8
Roxy Music – Michael Kulikowski 978-1-78952-335-5
Rush 1973 to 1982 – Richard James 978-1-78952-338-6
Sensational Alex Harvey Band – Peter Gallagher 978-1-7952-289-1
The Small Faces and The Faces – Andrew Darlington 978-1-78952-316-4
The Smashing Pumpkins – Matt Karpe 978-1-7952-291-4
The Smiths and Morrissey – Tommy Gunnarsson 978-1-78952-140-5
Soft Machine – Scott Meze 978-1078952-271-6
Sparks 1969-1979 – Chris Sutton 978-1-78952-279-2
Spirit – Rev. Keith A. Gordon – 978-1-78952- 248-8
Stackridge – Alan Draper 978-1-78952-232-7
Status Quo the Frantic Four Years – Richard James 978-1-78952-160-3
Steely Dan – Jez Rowden 978-1-78952-043-9

The Stranglers – Martin Hutchinson 978-1-78952-323-2
Talk Talk – Gary Steel 978-1-78952-284-6
Talking Heads – David Starkey 978-178952-353-9
Tears For Fears – Paul Clark – 978-178952-238-9
Thin Lizzy – Graeme Stroud 978-1-78952-064-4
Tool – Matt Karpe 978-1-78952-234-1
Toto – Jacob Holm-Lupo 978-1-78952-019-4
U2 – Eoghan Lyng 978-1-78952-078-1
UFO – Richard James 978-1-78952-073-6
Ultravox – Brian J. Robb 978-1-78952-330-0
Van Der Graaf Generator – Dan Coffey 978-1-78952-031-6
Van Halen – Morgan Brown – 9781-78952-256-3
Suzanne Vega – Lisa Torem 978-1-78952-281-5
Jack White And The White Stripes – Ben L. Connor 978-1-78952-303-4
The Who – Geoffrey Feakes 978-1-78952-076-7
Roy Wood and the Move – James R Turner 978-1-78952-008-8
Yes (new edition) – Stephen Lambe 978-1-78952-282-2
Neil Young 1963 to 1970 – Opher Goodwin 978-1-78952-298-3
Frank Zappa 1966 to 1979 – Eric Benac 978-1-78952-033-0
Warren Zevon – Peter Gallagher 978-1-78952-170-2
The Zombies – Emma Stott 978-1-78952-297-6
10CC – Peter Kearns 978-1-78952-054-5

Decades Series

The Bee Gees in the 1960s – Andrew Mon Hughes et al 978-1-78952-148-1
The Bee Gees in the 1970s – Andrew Mon Hughes et al 978-1-78952-179-5
Black Sabbath in the 1970s – Chris Sutton 978-1-78952-171-9
Britpop – Peter Richard Adams and Matt Pooler 978-1-78952-169-6
Phil Collins in the 1980s – Andrew Wild 978-1-78952-185-6
Alice CoOpher in the 1970s – Chris Sutton 978-1-78952-104-7
Alice CoOpher in the 1980s – Chris Sutton 978-1-78952-259-4
Curved Air in the 1970s – Laura Shenton 978-1-78952-069-9
Donovan in the 1960s – Jeff Fitzgerald 978-1-78952-233-4
Bob Dylan in the 1980s – Don Klees 978-1-78952-157-3
Brian Eno in the 1970s – Gary Parsons 978-1-78952-239-6
Faith No More in the 1990s – Matt Karpe 978-1-78952-250-1
Fleetwood Mac in the 1970s – Andrew Wild 978-1-78952-105-4
Fleetwood Mac in the 1980s – Don Klees 978-178952-254-9
Focus in the 1970s – Stephen Lambe 978-1-78952-079-8
Free and Bad Company in the 1970s – John Van der Kiste 978-1-78952-178-8
Genesis in the 1970s – Bill Thomas 978178952-146-7
George Harrison in the 1970s – Eoghan Lyng 978-1-78952-174-0

Kiss in the 1970s – Peter Gallagher 978-1-78952-246-4
Manfred Mann's Earth Band in the 1970s – John Van der Kiste 978178952-243-3
Marillion in the 1980s – Nathaniel Webb 978-1-78952-065-1
Van Morrison in the 1970s – Peter Childs – 978-1-78952-241-9
Mott the Hoople & Ian Hunter in the 1970s – John Van der Kiste 978-1-78-952-162-7
Pink Floyd In The 1970s – Georg Purvis 978-1-78952-072-9
Suzi Quatro in the 1970s – Darren Johnson 978-1-78952-236-5
Queen in the 1970s – James Griffiths 978-1-78952-265-5
Roxy Music in the 1970s – Dave Thompson 978-1-78952-180-1
Slade in the 1970s – Darren Johnson 978-1-78952-268-6
Status Quo in the 1980s – Greg Harper 978-1-78952-244-0
Tangerine Dream in the 1970s – Stephen Palmer 978-1-78952-161-0
The Sweet in the 1970s – Darren Johnson 978-1-78952-139-9
Uriah Heep in the 1970s – Steve Pilkington 978-1-78952-103-0
Van der Graaf Generator in the 1970s – Steve Pilkington 978-1-78952-245-7
Rick Wakeman in the 1970s – Geoffrey Feakes 978-1-78952-264-8
Yes in the 1980s – Stephen Lambe with David Watkinson 978-1-78952-125-2

Rock Classics Series

90125 by Yes – Stephen Lambe 978-1-78952-329-4
Bat Out Of Hell by Meatloaf – Geoffrey Feakes 978-1-78952-320-1
Bringing It All Back Home by Bob Dylan – Opher Goodwin 978-1-78952-314-0
Californication by Red Hot Chili Peppers - Matt Karpe 978-1-78952-348-5
Crime Of The Century by Supertramp – Steve Pilkington 978-1-78952-327-0
The Dreaming by Kate Bush – Peter Kearns 978-1-78952-341-6
Let It Bleed by The Rolling Stones – John Van der Kiste 978-1-78952-309-6
Pawn Hearts by Van Der Graaf Generator – Paolo Carnelli 978-1-78952-357-7
Purple Rain by Prince – Matt Karpe 978-1-78952-322-5
The White Album by The Beatles – Opher Goodwin 978-1-78952-333-1

On Screen Series

Carry On… – Stephen Lambe 978-1-78952-004-0
David Cronenberg – Patrick Chapman 978-1-78952-071-2
Doctor Who: The David Tennant Years – Jamie Hailstone 978-1-78952-066-8
James Bond – Andrew Wild 978-1-78952-010-1
Monty Python – Steve Pilkington 978-1-78952-047-7
Seinfeld Seasons 1 to 5 – Stephen Lambe 978-1-78952-012-5

Other Books

1967: A Year In Psychedelic Rock 978-1-78952-155-9
1970: A Year In Rock – John Van der Kiste 978-1-78952-147-4
1972: The Year Progressive Rock Ruled The World – Kevan Furbank 978-1-78952-288-4
1973: The Golden Year of Progressive Rock 978-1-78952-165-8

Eric Clapton Sessions – Andrew Wild 978-1-78952-177-1
Dark Horse Records – Aaron Badgley 978-1-78952-287-7
Derek Taylor: For Your Radioactive Children – Andrew Darlington 978-1-78952-038-5
Ghosts – Journeys To Post-Pop – Matthew Restall 978-1-78952-334-8
The Golden Age of Easy Listening – Derek Taylor 978-1-78952-285-3
The Golden Road: The Recording History of The Grateful Dead – John Kilbride 978-1-78952-156-6
Hoggin' The Page – Groudhogs The Classic Years – Martyn Hanson 978-1-78952-343-0
Iggy and The Stooges On Stage 1967-1974 – Per Nilsen 978-1-78952-101-6
Jon Anderson and the Warriors – the Road to Yes – David Watkinson 978-1-78952-059-0
Magic: The David Paton Story – David Paton 978-1-78952-266-2
Misty: The Music of Johnny Mathis – Jakob Baekgaard 978-1-78952-247-1
Musical Guide To Red By King Crimson – Andrew Keeling 978-1-78952-321-8
Nu Metal: A Definitive Guide – Matt Karpe 978-1-78952-063-7
Philip Lynott – Renegade – Alan Byrne 978-1-78952-339-3
Remembering Live Aid – Andrew Wild 978-1-78952-328-7
Thank You For The Days - Fans Of The Kinks Share 60 Years of Stories – Ed. Chris Kocher 978-1-78952-342-3
The Sonicbond On Track Sampler – 978-1-78952-190-0
The Sonicbond Progressive Rock Sampler (Ebook only) – 978-1-78952-056-9
Tommy Bolin: In and Out of Deep Purple – Laura Shenton 978-1-78952-070-5
Maximum Darkness – Deke Leonard 978-1-78952-048-4
The Twang Dynasty – Deke Leonard 978-1-78952-049-1

... and many more to come!

Would you like to write for Sonicbond Publishing?

At Sonicbond Publishing we are always on the look-out for authors, particularly for our two main series:

On Track. Mixing fact with in depth analysis, the On Track series examines the work of a particular musical artist or group. All genres are considered from easy listening and jazz to 60s soul to 90s pop, via rock and metal.

On Screen. This series looks at the world of film and television. Subjects considered include directors, actors and writers, as well as entire television and film series. As with the On Track series, we balance fact with analysis.

While professional writing experience would, of course, be an advantage the most important qualification is to have real enthusiasm and knowledge of your subject. First-time authors are welcomed, but the ability to write well in English is essential.

Sonicbond Publishing has distribution throughout Europe and North America, and all books are also published in E-book form. Authors will be paid a royalty based on sales of their book.

Further details are available from www.sonicbondpublishing.co.uk. To contact us, complete the contact form there or email info@sonicbondpublishing.co.uk